Many Germans were thrilled to see Hitler as the new ruler of the land, but many others were horrified.

Thousands of the brightest and best, who saw through Hitler's drama to his true evil nature, fled Germany for the United States. And there were none more fearful of the rise to supreme power of the new Führer than the German Jews.

"Everybody shook," one Jewish woman recalled of her and her Jewish friends' reaction the day Hitler became dictator. "As kids of 10, we shook, because we knew a terrible storm was coming."

A Background Note about *The Deadliest War*

What makes a war a *world* war? It is hard to imagine that every single country on Earth was fighting in World War II. However, by 1942 there were, in fact, very few nations that were not involved in one way or another. Even countries that did not send soldiers to fight often provided materials and resources. Some countries hid spies or protected war criminals; others reached out to help those who had been cruelly driven out of their homes. It is estimated that by the end of the war, 75 percent of all people living on the planet had been affected in some way by the six years of fighting.

The stunning magnitude of this war also made it a world war. More than 60 million people were killed, two-thirds of them innocent civilians. Hundreds of cities and towns were reduced to smoldering ruins. The cost of property damage worldwide was in the hundreds of billions of dollars. It was such a fierce and deadly war that it led Albert Einstein to believe that any war worse than this one would result in the end of civilization as we know it: "I know not with what weapons World War III will be fought," he commented, "but World War IV will be fought with sticks and stones."

World War II was, nonetheless, a war fought to make the world a better place. It was a necessary war. It was a long conflict that demanded tremendous sacrifice from those who were not only loyal to their countries but also loyal to the fair and just treatment of humankind.

THE DEADLIEST WAR

The Story of World War II

MARK THOMAS

 THE TOWNSEND LIBRARY

THE DEADLIEST WAR:
The Story of World War II

TP THE TOWNSEND LIBRARY

For more titles in the Townsend Library,
visit our website: **www.townsendpress.com**

Illustrations © 2011 by Hal Taylor

0 9 8 7 6 5 4 3 2 1

Townsend Press, Inc.
439 Kelley Drive
West Berlin, NJ 08091
permissions@townsendpress.com

ISBN-13: 978-1-59194-228-3
ISBN-10: 1-59194-228-4

Library of Congress Control Number:
2010939929

CONTENTS

CHAPTER 1

In 1908, a young man wandered aimlessly around Austria, a country bordering Germany. Penniless and with no real direction in his life, the young man slept in homeless shelters and ate in soup kitchens. Now and then he would work an odd job to earn just enough money to get by, but he preferred to think of himself as a misunderstood artist. Finally he applied to a famous art school in Vienna, certain that his talent would get him accepted. Although he was a high-school dropout who had barely passed his classes, he didn't think any of that would matter at an art institute.

Much to his surprise, however, the school rejected his application. When the young man stormed into the school, demanding an explanation, school officials did not try to soften the blow. They said that while some of his drawings of buildings were decent, his drawings of people looked lifeless and lacked any kind of human warmth. This made the young man bitter and angry, and he often complained to his few friends that no one appreciated true talent anymore. If his friends disagreed with him even slightly, he would often scream at them and then refuse to ever speak to them again.

His dreams of being an artist ruined, the young man turned his attention elsewhere. He had always been fascinated by Germany, the powerful country next door to Austria. Germans were tall and strong—and fiercely proud of their country and their ancestry; they had a history of not letting anyone push them around or tell them they weren't good enough. To the young man, there was nothing more admirable than this. And so he studied and read everything he could find about German leaders and German history.

In particular, the young man became obsessed with the idea that other races and other Europeans were ruining the "pure" race of German people. He pored over writings that used half-truths, exaggerations, and outright lies to convince readers that only those of pure German ancestry were good enough to remain in Germany. This kind of writing is known as "propaganda," and its main goal is to brainwash people into believing something that isn't true. The young man had originally been interested in the truths of German history, but the more propaganda he read, the more interested he became in the lies. Worse still, he believed them.

Beware the Jewish Snake! The young man carried a pamphlet with this title as he wandered the streets of Vienna. Who were these horrible Jews? he wondered, somewhat bewildered, as he stared into strangers' faces. When he had made a meager living selling his art, one of his main buyers had been a Jewish man who had even become a friend. The Austrians were more welcoming of Jews and people from other cultures and other countries than the German people were. In Austria, thousands of Jews lived happy, successful lives and offered a great deal to their communities as doctors, lawyers, tradesmen, and teachers.

But now the young man had read enough propaganda to come to believe that Jews were not what they presented themselves to be. It was all a cover-up. The literature and pamphlets pointed out again and again that it was the Jews who had killed Jesus Christ, and though they may seem kind and thoughtful, they have a hidden plan. In fact, the book that the young man had just finished reading warned that Jews were attempting to take over the entire world! In one pamphlet, pictures of "typical Jews" had been drawn—scowling, big-nosed, wicked-looking men with long beards and evil eyes. Now the young man spotted a few older men who looked a bit like this, and he followed them, observing them carefully and remembering all the propaganda he had read.

Before long, the young man came to a conclusion that he would often say aloud. At first he would say it to his few friends, trembling with anger if they disagreed. Later, he would declare it a bit more confidently to political groups gathered in beer halls. And eventually he would stand before many thousands of Germans who would cheer him as he shrieked in his high-pitched and furious voice: "The Jews are definitely a race, but they are not human!"

The young man's name was Adolf Hitler.

Hitler's love affair with Germany continued for some years, and by the time he was 24, he left Austria for Germany. Hitler was disgusted that many Austrians didn't seem to care if those of different races, religions, and nationalities settled in their country. How, Hitler wondered, could Austrians keep their race pure if they mingled with outsiders? In time, Hitler decided he would go to "the Fatherland," as he called Germany, and find a way to show his support of it. He would get his first chance in 1914.

On June 28, 1914, a young terrorist from Serbia (a country south of Austria) killed the heir to Austria's throne after years of disagreements between the two countries about land rights. Immediately, Germany pushed Austria to declare war on Serbia. Then one country after another declared war. Russia joined in the fight to support Serbia, and then Germany jumped aboard to defend Austria. France and England, both friends of the Russians, soon joined the war to help their ally. And when

German submarines, known as "U-boats," attacked American ships that were taking food and supplies to British armies, the United States mobilized against Germany. It seemed as if the whole world was at war—and it was. This was World War I.

Hitler was so thrilled with the idea of becoming a German soldier that he literally fell to his knees, wept, and thanked the heavens when Germany declared war on Russia. Immediately, Hitler enlisted. All the young German soldiers were certain that this would be a short war; after all, Germany was so powerful, and their military was enormous. Who could possibly beat them?

World War I was not a short war, however. It dragged on for four years, and millions of people were killed. It was a particularly deadly war, because it was the first one in which new vehicles, such as tanks and airplanes, were utilized, as well as the first war where both sides used poisonous gas extensively. Machine-gun fire was so feared that many soldiers dug deep trenches into the ground to give them some kind of protection from the constant rain of bullets. This "trench warfare" was muddy and lice-infested. And, depending on the time of year, it was either scorchingly hot or numbingly cold.

Hitler, by all accounts, was an odd soldier. He dressed sloppily and avoided friendships with other soldiers. When there was the opportunity to take a break and go drinking in a beer hall with his fellow soldiers, Hitler remained behind, choosing instead to read German histories in his tent. (Once, when he was younger, Hitler had gotten drunk with friends. He had awakened the next morning sprawled on the side of the road, an old farmer kicking him to see if he was alive. From that point on, Hitler never touched alcohol again.) As always, Hitler was quick-tempered and inclined to cut off anyone who disagreed with him on even the smallest matters.

Although he was a loner, Hitler was dedicated to the war. He never complained, never took leave when it was offered, and never shied away from the duties assigned to him, regardless of how dangerous they might be. And, miraculously, time and time again he avoided getting injured—even in the deadliest battles. Hitler was awarded medals for his service and bravery. However, he was never promoted to the rank of an officer. Because of his unfriendliness, other officers felt he would not have the ability to inspire and lead soldiers.

Then Hitler's amazing luck at avoiding war injuries ran out. In 1916, he was shot in the leg, an injury that would give him a lifelong limp. After recuperating, he visited Berlin, the capital of Germany, and was stunned by how many people were speaking out against the war. Hitler glared furiously at those who were criticizing the German and Austrian troops' efforts. Sometimes he even trailed them to see where they lived. What Germans *dared* to be foes of the German army? Hitler thought he knew.

"It is the Jews and the gypsies!" he snarled to an acquaintance one evening. "It is those who have come here from somewhere else. They have no sense of national pride!"

To Hitler, "nationalism," total and unconditional support of one's country, was more important than anything else. He scorned the gypsies, mostly from Romania, who were a free-spirited people that roamed throughout Europe. Because they spoke their own language and were dark-skinned, Hitler felt they had no right to live among the "pure" Germans he so admired. And the Jews, Hitler often noted, were a people who had been on the move for thousands of years. Throughout history, they had been expelled from more than seventy-five countries. They belonged nowhere, Hitler firmly believed. And they most certainly did not belong in Germany.

Angry and disillusioned by the indifference of many Berliners, Hitler returned to the war as soon as he was well enough. He still believed Germany would win the war, and he wanted to be on the frontlines when they did. However, eighteen months after returning to the war, he was temporarily blinded by poisonous gas and was once again hospitalized in Germany.

Hitler strained to hear the whispers and low conversations the medical staff carried on about the war. "Disaster . . . must surrender . . . doomed . . . the end." Although Hitler refused to believe that Germany was losing, one bitter November morning, an elderly pastor walked into the hospital and announced the news.

"Germany and Austria have fallen," he said quietly. "The war is over."

Hitler clenched his hands into fists. His sight was returning, but he felt no joy in it. He hated thinking of his beloved Germany in defeat, imagining its people broken and discouraged.

"There followed terrible days and even worse nights," Hitler would later write about that time. "I knew that all was lost. . . . In these nights hatred grew in me, hatred for those responsible for this deed."

Germany had been soundly defeated. Now, adding insult to injury, they were going to be punished for starting a war that had killed millions of people and had caused great destruction. Furthermore, the German government would not be allowed to participate in the drawing up of the punishment—France, England, and the United States would decide what was best.

Germany's fate was outlined in a document called the Treaty of Versailles. The first order of business was to make certain that Germany would never again be able to start a war. Doing this was easy enough: simply strip Germany of its military power. The Germans had had eleven million soldiers during World War I. Now they were forced to reduce that to a laughable 100,000. All the new weapons, such as submarines, fighter planes, and battleships, were taken out of Germany.

Next, Germany was forced to give up lands it had taken over and return them to France and Poland. Finally, Germany was slapped with a gigantic fine in order to repay its European enemies for damage that had been done to their countries during the war. Some of this repayment was in the form of resources, such as coal and agricultural products. The German government was instructed to pay the equivalent of nearly thirty-three billion dollars, an astronomical sum in 1919.

The German government could not refuse to meet any of the demands and could not stall in hopes of buying more time. Doing so could mean losing Germany entirely. Many felt that the main goal of the Treaty of Versailles was to humiliate and embarrass Germany in front of the entire world. That goal was achieved.

As can be imagined, many Germans were extremely bitter about this turn of events. The war had left most Germans poor, ragged, and defeated, and now things were about to get even worse.

There was, possibly, no one angrier than Adolf Hitler. Not only was Hitler angry at the Jews, who he felt had secretly worked together to bring Germany to ruin; he was also very upset with the German government. In his opinion, the government had been too quick to agree to surrender. He believed the government should have fought to the death! Anything other than that was cowardly, and, to Adolf Hitler, there was no room for cowardice in Germany. It was time for change. And it was at this point that Hitler began thinking that, just maybe, he was the man destined to make that change.

It is, perhaps, hard to imagine how an unfriendly, bitter man with a limp in his walk and a chip on his shoulder could ultimately become one of the most powerful and most feared leaders in the entire world.

It all began with a speech.

One evening, Hitler decided to visit a meeting of the German Workers' Party, a political group that, like Hitler, was unhappy with the current German government. Hitler sat quietly in the back of the room, listening to different speakers. He was not particularly impressed by any of them, but as he stood up to leave, a young man began presenting the idea of splitting up parts of Germany and turning the parts into separate countries. Hitler stopped in his tracks. *Divide Germany?* Hitler shook with rage and burst out in anger against the man who had spoken.

The entire room turned to listen. Amazingly, Hitler spoke for nearly twenty minutes, and no one interrupted. In fact, the group sat spellbound, drawn in by this stranger's hypnotic glare, his fiery words, and his emotional, almost hysterical, voice.

When Hitler finished with a flourish and turned abruptly to leave, one of the members rushed over to him and handed him a small book that contained the group's beliefs and goals.

"I hope you will read this, sir. We could use somebody with your passion," the member said politely.

Hitler dismissed him with a harsh laugh. Why would he care about this group's ideas? Nonetheless, he took the book.

Much later that night, Adolf Hitler placed the book carefully on his bookshelf. He had begun reading it reluctantly, but now he had read every word. He was amazed by how similar the beliefs of the German Workers' Party were to his own. The party saw a future where the military would be returned to its previous glory, and where Germans would be bursting with nationalist pride. And, to Hitler's great approval, the party agreed that "undesirables," the Jews, had no place in Germany.

Hitler sat up the rest of the night thinking. A small political party that shared his beliefs was already in place. It would require immense work and strong, perhaps even cruel, direction, but Hitler believed he could turn this party into a movement. It would be an overpowering, thunderous political party made up of working-class people—not spineless politicians. The movement this party would create would transform Germany into the most awesome and feared country on Earth.

Perhaps he had failed at art, at friendships, and even at war, but before sunrise on that fateful night, September 12, 1919, Adolf Hitler resolved that he would not fail again. He would become a leader.

"It was the most decisive resolve of my life," Hitler would later write. "From here there was and could be no turning back."

CHAPTER 2

"**H**e's a joke, I tell you. This Hitler is of no importance," a young Jewish man in Munich, Germany, said impatiently as he sat in a café drinking tea with a group of friends in 1930.

"I wouldn't be so sure," a thin man with nervous eyes said carefully. "He and his party received nearly twenty percent of the vote this time around. And it certainly doesn't look as though he's planning on slowing down his efforts."

An older Jewish man with a long gray beard just smiled and shook his head.

"Yes, I would say there's nothing much to worry about," he said. "Every so often a leader comes along shouting hatred of Jews. Some people agree with him, and some do not, and before long he disappears. Hitler is no different."

"But he *is* different," the thin man insisted. "He doesn't just hate us; he wants to destroy us. Every one of us."

"Don't you see how ridiculous that is, though?" the young man said with a laugh. "No one man, not even Hitler with his ridiculous group of brown-shirted Nazis, can destroy an entire people. Why, even if he managed to wipe out German Jews, there are millions more living in Poland, in the Soviet Union, and beyond."

The thin, nervous man sighed and looked out the window. Across the street was a nicer café, the place where he and his friends used to go. Now, however, a big sign on the door read "Nein Juden" (German for "No Jews"). It was a sign that was becoming more and more common.

"I wouldn't be so sure," he repeated quietly.

Since Hitler had stumbled upon the German Workers' Party years earlier, he had been extremely busy and focused. Hitler's hypnotic and persuasive style of speaking impressed the party members so much that they immediately appointed him as the official party spokesman. This put Hitler in front of so many people that most Germans just assumed that Hitler was the party's leader. Impressed both with himself and with the way people were beginning to see him, less than a year later Hitler simply declared himself the leader of the party.

"I am the Führer!" Hitler roared to the growing party, *Führer* being the German word for "leader." It was a title that Hitler would demand others use for him until the day he died.

Perhaps because he had often been ignored or disregarded growing up, Hitler had developed a sharp sense of exactly what *did* get people's attention. For that reason, Hitler first decided to change the name of the party to *National Socialist German Workers' Party* (shortened to *Nazi Party*). "Socialist" meant that all people were equal, but adding "national" pointed out that only true Germans were equal—no one else. Germans who still felt the sting of the world laughing at them for losing World War I wanted nothing more than to join a party that would glorify their country and its people.

Next, Hitler looked for a symbol, something eye-catching to put on the party's flags and posters.

"It must be a symbol of our own struggle," Hitler told his fellow Nazis.

Hitler settled on the swastika. It was not a new symbol; it had been used by different cultures and peoples for more than 9,000 years. Throughout the ages, it had been a symbol of power, strength, sunlight, and good luck. Even the ancient word *swastika* meant "to be good."

But now, all that would change.

The Nazis designed their flag to be bright red, with a white circle and a large black swastika in the center. Hitler explained the design: "In red we see the social idea of the movement, in white the nationalistic idea, in the swastika the mission of the struggle for the victory of the Aryan man . . . which as such always has been and always will be anti-Semitic."

What had symbolized life and happiness for thousands of years would now come to symbolize hatred and death.

As the weak German government grew more and more unpopular with Germans, the fierce Nazi party began drawing attention. By 1922, it had grown to 6,000 members, and in 1923 it swelled to 55,000. It was then, in 1923, that Hitler decided to make his move. Hitler had been impressed by how Italy's leader, Benito Mussolini, had simply marched into Rome with his followers and taken over the Italian government. Now, even though most Germans still had never heard of Hitler or the Nazis, Hitler vainly believed he could do the same.

On the night of November 8, 1923, Hitler and a group of armed Nazi soldiers (known as "the SS") stormed into a popular beer hall in Munich. Hitler jumped up onto a table and fired rifle shots at the ceiling, screaming, "The national revolution has broken out! . . . A new government will be formed at once. The barracks of the *Reichswehr* [the German army] and those of the police are occupied. Both have rallied to the swastika."

In reality, neither had rallied to the swastika. However, Hitler knew that creating excitement was the first step. If, throughout the night, he could gather more and more supporters by lying to them about the start of a revolution, by dawn the real revolution would be under way.

The nearly 3,000 men in the beer hall stared angrily at this little man who ordered them to sit down and listen to him.

"No one is allowed to leave!" Hitler shrieked as some of the men dashed to exits through the kitchen.

As the SS blocked the doorways, Hitler began to speak to the crowd. Almost instantly, a hush fell over the rowdy group. One man, a professor at the University of Munich, later wrote about Hitler's speech:

"I cannot remember in my entire life such a change in the attitude of a crowd in a few minutes, almost a few seconds," he recalled. "Hitler had turned them inside out, as one turns a glove inside out, with a few sentences. It had almost something of hocus-pocus, or magic about it."

Magic or not, Hitler's famous "Beer Hall Putsch," as it came to be known, fell flat. (*Putsch* means "punch" or, more generally, "uprising.") Though a storm of 2,000 Nazis and supporters marched through Munich the next day shouting about revolution, the police overpowered them. More than a dozen Nazis and several policemen were killed, and Hitler was sentenced to five years in prison. However, because of growing public sympathy for his beliefs, Hitler would serve only six months.

As Hitler sat in prison, word of his attempted takeover began spreading rapidly throughout Germany. Before long, Adolf Hitler was thought of as something of a hero—a brave man who had stood up to the failing government in an attempt to make his beloved Germany a better place. This time, Hitler's failure was turning him into a success.

Hitler did not waste his time in prison. He wrote a book, *Mein Kampf (My Struggle)*, that outlined many of his political and personal views. In many ways, it was a rambling, confusing, and poorly written book. However, one point was made very clear: Jews were the enemy, and they must be conquered. Hitler went to great lengths in *Mein Kampf* to divide people into categories based almost completely upon what they looked like. At the very top was what Hitler called the "Aryan" race. These were the blond, blue-eyed Germans.

"The Aryan is the supreme form of human," Hitler wrote. "The Aryan is the master race."

Far below this "master race" were people of color, gypsies, mentally and physically handicapped people, homosexuals, and, at the very bottom, Jews. Drawing upon his old beliefs in the propaganda he had read, Hitler warned that Jews were secretly working to take over the world and destroy it with evil. "The personification of the devil as the symbol of all evil assumes the living shape of the Jew," Hitler warned.

How did he plan to combat this evil? Hitler recommended building and expanding the master race while getting rid of the unfit races. To accomplish this, more of what Hitler referred to as "living space" would be needed. Germany would need to acquire both Austria and countries to the east, such as Poland and parts of the Soviet Union. Once Germany began expanding, the pure and strong master race would be on its way to world domination. In Hitler's opinion, this was not just something *he* wanted—it was what *God* wanted.

Finally, Hitler laughed at democratic governments and called them weak and destined to fail. He believed that countries should be ruled by dictators. One man making the decisions and laws for everyone would serve to make a country stronger and more unified. He believed that electing leaders was a huge mistake.

Even so, Hitler realized that he would have to bide his time and be patient with the current weak government. He was not above going against his own beliefs in order to rise to power. His Beer Hall Putsch had not worked. If he could not take over the government by force as Mussolini had done in Italy, he would play by the rules and get elected. It might take years, but one day he would be dictator. One day, the Nazi Party would come to power, and after that, the master race would reign.

Mein Kampf clearly spelled out the evil that was Adolf Hitler. It was so personal, so angry, and so detailed that, years later, Hitler claimed that he wished he had not revealed so much of himself in it.

It was a clear warning of what was to come. But in 1925, no one took it very seriously.

* * *

Some quiet years followed for Hitler and the Nazis. For a while, the German economy grew stronger, so revolution and the idea of overthrowing the government were not as appealing to Germans. They preferred entertainment and beer halls to Hitler's angry speeches, and some Germans even poked fun at Hitler, comparing him to the comic American film star Charlie Chaplin. It was a comparison that did not amuse Hitler. Perhaps more than anything, Hitler hated for anyone to laugh at him.

However, Hitler worked steadily, and he gradually began gathering more followers. He knew that the German government was bound to become unpopular again at some point. And that point arrived when the stock market crashed in 1929. Although the crash took place in the United States, it affected countries worldwide, and it was particularly hard on Germany.

Suddenly, Germans who had been enjoying the good life found their bank accounts wiped out and their savings gone. Inflation reached ridiculous heights; money had so little value that some people burned it for fuel or used it as wallpaper. Now Germans were looking for anything—or anyone— to turn the terrible times around. As before, Germans blamed the government—how could the government have let this happen?

In stepped Adolf Hitler to the rescue.

The Nazi Party had been slow to gain any real political power, but as soon as the stock market crashed, Germans began electing more and more Nazis to positions in the government, believing that a fierce leader like Hitler might have the answers. By 1930, nearly 20 percent of Germans supported the Nazi Party, and 107 Nazis were elected to the *Reichstag* (the German law-making body). Nazis celebrated by storming through the streets of Berlin and smashing the windows of Jewish-owned businesses. It was a warning of what was to come.

Many Germans were just looking for someone to blame for the hard times, and Jews seemed as good a target as anyone. Hitler was quick to pounce on this opportunity to remind Germans of his plan to remove Jews from the Fatherland and rebuild Germany as the home of the master race.

Still, many Germans continued to dismiss Hitler as something of a harmless lunatic. Who on earth would take this shouting little man with the funny moustache and crazy ideas about a pure race seriously? There were plenty of Germans who were close friends with Jewish people, who were even relatives of Jews. Who, they continued to wonder, would ever support such an unthinkable plan? It seemed ridiculous—laughable.

But as life in Germany continued on a downward spiral, the popularity of Hitler and the Nazis rose higher and higher. Hitler was a master at telling people exactly what they wanted to hear, and now he painted a dramatic picture of a new German *Reich* ("empire"), the "Third Reich," that would last one thousand years and vault Germany to a position of world domination. Never again would anyone humiliate Germany! Never again would Germans be forced to pay unfair debts and give up their military strength. Never!

And by 1932, the Nazis were the strongest party in Germany. The July elections put 230 Nazis into the Reichstag.

"In the Third Reich, every German girl will find a husband!" Hitler shouted, his dark eyes glittering as tremendous crowds cheered for him.

Hitler promised everything from husbands to jobs to world power—and people across Germany believed him. Many who had questioned him in the past were awestruck by Hitler's dynamic speaking and were overwhelmed by the Nazi display of strength and national pride. It contrasted vividly with Germany's depressed state.

At the time, the German government had two leaders: a president and a chancellor. When the chancellor resigned in 1932 due to political pressure, the president, Hindenburg, reluctantly appointed Hitler to be the new chancellor. Hindenburg didn't like Hitler, but Hitler was now the most popular leader in Germany; Hindenburg had little choice—the German people demanded it.

Once he became chancellor, Hitler got Hindenburg to sign orders that pardoned Nazi prisoners and allowed for the arrest and conviction of anyone suspected of criticizing the government. He went on to persuade the Reichstag to give up its right to make laws for the country. Since this involved changing Germany's constitution, approval by a two-thirds majority was required—and in order to get that majority, votes from members other than Nazis were needed. When the law passed on March 24, 1933, everything was in place for Adolf Hitler to take control of Germany. He had accomplished this peacefully and legally—without firing a shot or breaking a law.

Now, Hitler simply sat back and waited. Hindenburg was an old man, and he was in very poor health. His death would give Hitler the final move he needed in this complicated game of political chess that he had been playing for more than a decade. On August 2, 1934, Hindenburg died, and Hitler pounced. Instantly, he assumed the office of president as well as chancellor, using his SS men to threaten anyone who opposed this move. In addition, Hitler became commander in chief of Germany's armed forces, and he altered the traditional oath so that members swore their allegiance not to Germany but to him personally.

"We've done it! We've done it!" he screamed happily to a frenzied crowd of Nazi followers.

About two weeks later, 95 percent of Germany's registered voters went to the polls, and with a vote of nearly 85 percent confirmed Hitler as their leader.

With the official approval not only of President Hindenburg and the Reichstag but also of the German voters, Adolf Hitler had realized his dream of becoming dictator of Germany. Now, Hitler and his Nazi government would make every decision for the people of Germany. The people would remain powerless and without a voice, except in shouts of "Heil Hitler!"

Many Germans were thrilled to see Hitler as the new ruler of the land, but many others were horrified. Thousands of the brightest and best, who saw through Hitler's drama to his true evil nature, fled Germany for the United States. And there were none more fearful of the rise to supreme power of the new Führer than the German Jews.

"Everybody shook," one Jewish woman recalled of her and her Jewish friends' reaction the day Hitler became dictator. "As kids of 10, we shook, because we knew a terrible storm was coming."

CHAPTER 3

Hitler wasted no time in making life a living hell for Jews or for anyone who questioned his leadership. Over the next several years, he and his police organization, called "the Gestapo," made certain that all the new laws and rules that Hitler put into place were followed to the letter. Those who stepped out of line were publicly beaten or imprisoned—or worse.

As the Gestapo marched through city streets or roared into villages on motorcycles, Jews often hid inside their homes, hoping to remain unnoticed. Hitler had instructed his police to humiliate Jewish people in any and every way possible. Violence was rewarded. It became commonplace for the Gestapo to ransack Jewish businesses. Respected rabbis were dragged out of synagogues by their hair as people looked on and laughed. Jewish children were lined up and marched out of schools at gunpoint.

Hitler was particularly fond of using his Hitler Youth organization, composed of boys age 15 to 18, to harass Jews. In fact, all non-Jewish German boys and girls from age 10 to 18 were required to join the student organization appropriate to their age and gender. They wore military uniforms and were praised for being the future of Aryan Germany and the new promise of the master race. Hitler encouraged the older children to treat the younger ones as cruelly, and even brutally, as necessary in order to weed out the weaker or "unfit" children.

"The weak must be chipped away," Hitler explained matter-of-factly. "I want young men and women who can suffer pain! A young German must be as swift as a greyhound, as tough as leather, and as hard as Krupp's steel."

But most important for the future of Nazi Germany, the student organizations provided a way to brainwash the younger generation to worship Hitler and to despise Jews. Once the young people were thoroughly trained, they were assigned missions. Hitler favored using teens for humiliating the most learned and respected Jews. With the Gestapo standing nearby to ensure order, children as young as 10 forced Jewish doctors, lawyers, and professors into the streets.

"Down on your hands and knees!" the children would shout, prodding the adults with sticks. "Scrub these streets until they shine, you Jews!"

While people gathered around to jeer and yell insults, the children smugly watched their "prisoners" clean city streets with pages torn from books written by Jewish authors.

As the years went by, Hitler systematically took away all rights from German Jews. They could no longer own telephones, cars, or even bicycles. Their children were denied education. Their bank accounts and personal belongings were seized by the Nazi government. Large signs reading "Don't Buy From Jews! Jews Are Our Misfortune!" were placed on the doors of Jewish-owned businesses, and Germans obediently boycotted the businesses until the stores went bankrupt.

It may be difficult to understand how the German people apparently so easily turned against the Jews and followed Hitler's lead. One important reason for this was that Hitler turned Germany's poor economic condition around in an astoundingly short period of time. For all of Hitler's evil, he was also a tireless worker who was devoted to making life better—at least for non-Jewish Germans. In barely three years, while the rest of the world was still reeling from the Great Depression, Hitler managed to sharply reduce unemployment, rebuild the military, create many new industries, and even begin building a national highway that would connect all the people of Germany.

In addition, the Nazis completely controlled everything Germans read or heard on the radio (there was no television yet). Again and again, Germans were told that the Jews were to blame both for the loss of World War I and for all of Germany's troubles since then. And now that the Jews were being punished and denied rights, wasn't life better for all Germans? During this time, countless outrageous lies about Jews appeared in the daily papers. Jews, Germans were told, practiced witchcraft, intentionally spread disease, and even killed children. In time, Germans began to believe the propaganda—just as Hitler had as a young man.

Hitler had chosen his friend Joseph Goebbels to be director of propaganda. Goebbels was a mean-spirited little man, barely five feet tall, whose love of Hitler was overshadowed only by his hatred of Jews. Goebbels made weekly national radio addresses in which he told Germans that Jews were secretly connected worldwide and that they were currently putting together a specific plan to destroy Germany. He went on to explain that Germany had no choice but to wage deadly war against the Jews.

All along, Goebbels was well aware that nearly everything he was saying about Jewish people was a lie. He had studied propaganda for a long time, and he knew exactly what he was doing.

"If you tell a lie big enough and keep repeating it, people will eventually come to believe it," Goebbels once wrote.

And by 1938, Germans so thoroughly believed the lies that when a young Jewish man shot and killed a German diplomat, the country exploded in violence against Jews. The Gestapo and the SS crashed into thousands of Jewish homes and business with axes and burning torches. Furniture was smashed to bits, and personal belongings were heaped in the streets and set on fire. Non-Jewish Germans joined in the rioting and helped point out Jewish-owned businesses. So many glass storefronts were shattered that the fateful night of November 9, 1938, came to be known as *Kristallnacht*, or "Night of Broken Glass."

Before morning, nearly every synagogue in Germany had been either badly damaged or burned to the ground. German officers handed rocks to village children and instructed them to break as many stained-glass windows in the synagogues as possible. Cemeteries behind the synagogues were dug up, rotting caskets were thrown into the streets, and tombstones were broken into bits with sledgehammers.

By the time the rioting ended, nearly 100 Jews had been killed. More than 20,000 Jews, mostly men, were arrested for no reason, crammed into freezing cattle cars, and shipped off to remote labor camps, where many of them would die from disease or starvation. Many Jews, realizing that there was no other way to escape the brutal treatment by the Germans, took their own lives during the Night of Broken Glass.

It's important to remember, however, that not *all* Germans readily bought the Nazi lies. Many pitied their Jewish friends and tried to find ways to help them. But those caught aiding Jewish people were punished severely. Even friendships were forbidden. If a German was caught spending time with a Jew, he or she might be marched through the streets all day wearing a large sign announcing "I am friends with the enemy—a Jew!" Still, many non-Jewish people would risk their lives throughout World War II to help Jews escape the terror of the Nazis.

In 1938, Hitler took his first step toward conquering Europe and gaining "living space" for the master race: He overtook Austria (which had been separate from Hungary since World War I). The takeover was not very difficult. Many Austrians had already joined the Nazi party and had been looking forward to becoming part of Germany. Although the chancellor of Austria, naturally, opposed it, he was too afraid of Hitler to fight back. In the end, Austria was added to Germany without one gun ever being fired.

Although it would seem that other European countries would have been worried about Germany's invasion of Austria, none of them came to Austria's aid. France did not want to get involved in another conflict so soon after World War I. And Italy's dictator, Mussolini, approved of Hitler's aggression and sent him a message telling him so.

"Tell Mussolini I will never forget him for this!" Hitler responded, thrilled that another dictator was on his side. "I shall stick by him even if the whole world gangs up on him!"

Meanwhile, England continued to believe that Hitler was not really a threat. Britain's prime minister, Neville Chamberlain, assured Europeans and the rest of the world that he would simply sit down with Hitler and work out a friendly agreement. The two met in Munich in late 1938, and Hitler promised to invade no other lands.

"In spite of the hardness and ruthlessness I thought I saw in his face," Chamberlain claimed, "I got the impression that here was a man who could be relied upon when he had given his word."

With that, Chamberlain returned to England, proudly announcing that there would be "peace for our time."

Less than a year later, however, Hitler broke the promise he had never intended to keep, and he invaded Poland. England and France had no choice but to come to Poland's aid. World War II had begun.

Jews in Austria and Poland now faced the same terror as German Jews. By 1940, Hitler had set up a number of concentration camps throughout Poland and Germany. Originally, these were prison camps, used mostly for holding political prisoners and enemies of the Nazis. Over time, however, more and more Jews were sent to these camps to be worked, tortured, or starved to death.

Hitler encouraged the Gestapo and the SS to kill as many Jews as possible, either by rounding them up and sending them to camps or by simply shooting them. However, Hitler knew that these murders must be kept secret from the rest of the world. Therefore, his concentration camps were built in remote and isolated areas. The shootings took place deep in the heavy forests.

What Hitler was doing, however, began to trickle back to Jews in rumors and difficult-to-believe stories. Sometimes, very rarely, prisoners escaped. Even more rarely, someone who was shot and left for dead survived and made his or her way out of the forests. Sketchy tales of the horror drifted from town to town. Before long, when the rumble of the Gestapo's motorcycles or the marching thunder of the SS's boots neared villages and towns, panicked Jewish people had only one thought: *Hide.*

A young Jewish girl named Luncia Gamzer, who lived in the Polish city of Lvov, remembered the nightmare of hiding. When she was barely 8, Nazi soldiers began storming into Lvov, destroying Jewish-owned businesses and rounding up groups of Jews, who were then packed into the back of trucks and never seen again. Luncia knew that some of these people were taken into the woods and murdered—she had heard the rifle shots one day when she had been gathering mushrooms along a forest path.

Luncia recalled the first time her mother had told her to hide. A tall German soldier had simply walked into the Gamzers' house in the middle of the day and asked to be fed. Luncia peeked through a crack in the closet door at her terrified mother, whose hands shook as she handed the soldier soup and tea.

"These are nice pots," the soldier had said, looking at the family's only cookware. "Clean them up. I'm taking them with me."

Luncia realized then that the Nazis would take whatever they wanted. And the next time the Gestapo came to the Gamzers' door, it wasn't for soup pots.

"Open up!" the Gestapo shouted in the middle of the night. "All Jewish children must come with us! If any are caught hiding, your entire family will be shot immediately!"

Luncia's mother and father knew that hiding their daughter was her only chance. If she left with the Gestapo, it meant certain death.

"Quickly," Luncia's father whispered, "in the bathroom!"

Luncia crouched behind the bathtub. She heard her father slide a large wardrobe in front of the bathroom door. Luncia sat in the dark holding her breath and hearing her heart pound in her ears. "Please, God," she prayed silently. "Please don't let him find me."

"Your children! Now!" the Gestapo soldier yelled as he charged into the Gamzers' home.

"We . . . we have no children," Luncia's father stammered.

The soldier walked slowly around the home. Luncia could hear his heavy footsteps getting closer and closer. Finally he stopped. He was right in front of the covered door.

"What is this?" he yelled. "Where is she?"

Luncia felt as though she was going to be sick. He must have noticed the door. Then she heard her mother.

"That's an old picture of our daughter. But they already took her away."

Luncia realized that the soldier had seen the picture of her on the wall near the bathroom door. There was a long silence, and then the soldier said, with a sneer in his voice, "It looks like you *used* to have a pretty child."

There was a stomping of boots and the slamming of a door. The Gestapo soldier was gone.

Not long after this incident, all of the Jews in Lvov were ordered to move to one tiny corner of the city. This Jewish ghetto would make it easier for soldiers both to keep an eye on Jews and to round them up when sending them to camps or to their deaths in the forests. At every corner, every bridge, and every tunnel, the Gestapo stood with their rifles in hand. Anyone caught trying to escape was shot on the spot.

Luncia's father was a bit luckier than others. He was a successful businessman, so he was considered "useful" to the Nazis. He was allowed to leave the ghetto every day to go to work in the better part of the city. While he was not allowed to keep even a quarter of the money he earned, his job gave him and his family some hope.

Day by day, the Gestapo rounded up more people. In particular, they focused on children, the elderly, and the sick. Anyone who could not work hard was of no importance to the Nazis. As Hitler often said, they were only taking up space they didn't deserve. Luncia and her parents often hid in a muddy hole they had dug beneath the porch of the small house where they and four other families lived.

But Luncia's father knew their hiding place would eventually be discovered.

One morning, he told Luncia that he had a plan to get her out of the ghetto and to safety. A family friend, a Polish Christian woman, was willing to hide Luncia in her home in the city. It was a crime punishable by death, but this friend, like so many friends of Jews, was willing to risk her life. The woman had sent a message to Luncia's parents telling them to get Luncia to her father's office. The woman would then sneak Luncia back to her house late at night.

"You must hide beneath my coat tomorrow morning when I leave the ghetto," her father said. "It's the only way."

Luncia was sick with fear, but the next morning she did as her father told her. His long coat nearly touched the ground, and if she kept her footsteps in time with his, no one could tell she was hiding there. When her father reached the checkpoint where the Gestapo would check his pass to allow him out of the ghetto, Luncia once again held her breath. She stood as close as she could to her father, and he could feel her shaking.

Then something went wrong.

"Now! Show me your pass, you filthy Jew!" one of the soldiers was screaming at the man in front of her father.

"I know it's here somewhere," the man was saying desperately. "I just had it. . . . I . . ."

Without warning, there was a shattering rifle blast. Luncia heard the man fall heavily to the ground next to her father.

"He's going to shoot us all," Luncia thought in terror. It was not uncommon for the Nazi soldiers to lose their tempers and go on a shooting rampage, killing anyone within range. But suddenly her father was walking again. There was the rattling of papers, a brisk "Pass!" from a soldier, and they were out of the ghetto.

Luncia hid in her father's office all day. As it grew dark, her father knelt beside her and told her to be brave. He would have to leave her now.

"But when will I ever see you again?" Luncia asked, tears streaming down her cheeks.

There were tears in her father's eyes, too, but he tried to reassure her that everything would be all right. She must have hope. She must stay hidden.

Hide. It was a word Luncia, like thousands of other Jews, would hear, whisper to herself, and live by for nearly three years.

CHAPTER 4

How did this war, which was at first just between Germany and a few European countries, become a worldwide war? As in World War I, once countries began choosing sides, more and more countries became involved.

When France and Great Britain declared war on Germany after the invasion of Poland, all dominions of Great Britain (countries that were partly under British rule) were obligated to join the fight. These countries spanned the world: Canada, Australia, South Africa, India, and New Zealand. As a group, the countries that opposed Germany were called "the Allies" or "the Allied forces."

However, at first nothing much happened. France and England stalled for time in order to build up their armies. Hitler was eager for a war to begin, since he was confident that German forces could easily overpower the French and British armies. But when war was first declared in September 1939, German forces were too busy taking over Poland to focus on France and England.

The Polish people suddenly found themselves in a nightmare of war. The Soviet Union and Germany had made a secret agreement to split Poland up, with the Germans taking western Poland and the Soviets taking the eastern parts. Now, both countries attacked Poland at the same time. The Germans used a new kind of warfare that they had named *blitzkrieg*, meaning "lightning war." State-of-the-art tanks and aircraft zoomed across Poland, striking towns and cities before their residents could even figure out what was happening. Many Poles had never seen an airplane before, much less a superfast bomber screaming through the skies.

The Polish army rushed to put some sort of counterattack together. But the army's methods of warfare were so outdated that some German soldiers actually burst into loud laughter when they saw the enemy approaching. Many Polish soldiers still rode on horseback and carried swords. The few guns they used were rusty antiques compared with the German high-powered rifles and machine guns. Yet the Poles rode bravely into battle to defend their country. They were slaughtered mercilessly.

"Close your hearts to pity. Act brutally," Hitler had told his armies the night before they went into battle. The Nazi soldiers were happy to follow the Führer's orders.

The Poles fought bitterly, but they were terribly outnumbered and obviously overpowered. In the end, 200,000 Poles were killed or wounded, and

694,000 were captured as prisoners. Hitler believed that Poles, like Jews, were subhuman, so he had most of the Polish prisoners sent to concentration camps. Once Poland had been conquered, many of these camps were built in Poland, so Poles were literally prisoners in what had so recently been their own county.

Hitler disliked the Polish people mainly because he found their coloring to be too dark to fit into his idea of the perfect race. In other words, most Poles weren't blue-eyed and blond. Even so, he noticed that many of the children and babies looked "German enough." Without a second thought, Hitler ordered the kidnapping of Polish children. According to official Polish estimates, 200,000 Polish children were kidnapped by the Nazis between 1940 and 1945. These children were then adopted by German families and "Germanized." Horrified Polish parents who ran screaming after their children were shot in the streets and left unburied as a warning to other parents.

Years later, when World War II ended, many people would look back on this time and wonder why the Allies had not taken action sooner. Why were the Nazis allowed to unleash their blitzkrieg on Poland without any resistance from Britain and France? Both countries spent nearly half a year preparing for war without ever actually engaging in it. Britain formed a war cabinet and made sure its navy was in place in case of any attacks by German submarines. France built a series of underground forts all along its border and sat back, waiting. This time period was known as "the phony war," because no real fighting ever took place.

Hitler, on the other hand, wasted no time. As German troops jokingly referred to France's and Britain's lack of action as a "sitzkrieg," or "sitting war," Hitler was planning more attacks on smaller European countries. Bit by bit, he would chip away at Europe until Britain would stand alone as the only country not controlled by the Nazis. When that happened, Hitler believed, Britain would either surrender or crumble under the power of an awesome blitzkrieg. And on that day, the Nazis would control all of Europe. Adolf Hitler would be the most powerful dictator in the world.

On the other side of the world, a similar drama was unfolding. Like the Germans, the Japanese wanted more land, more resources, and more power. For many years and through many battles, Japan had attempted to take over China, but had acquired only small pieces of that large nation. As part of Germany's punishment at the end of World War I, Japan had been given Chinese territories previously held by the Germans. Many of these territories were islands in the Pacific, full of rich resources. This only made Japan hungry for more.

So at the same time that Hitler was building up his power in Germany in the mid-1930s, Japan was pushing farther and farther into China. First, the big Chinese city of Peiping (today called "Beijing") fell, and then Shanghai. Japan pressed on to Nanking, the Chinese capital. By 1939, Japan controlled many of China's coastal cities and in some places extended its control 500 miles inland, over important areas and rich farmland.

How was this possible? Looking at a map, one can see that Japan is just a group of small islands. Next to its neighbor China, Japan looks like little more than a sliver. Wouldn't China be able to overwhelm the Japanese with sheer manpower? Didn't the Chinese even fight back?

In reality, the Chinese fought bravely, refusing to surrender even when there was no hope. However, much like the German army, the Japanese army was far more advanced than its enemy's. And, also like the Nazis, the Japanese soldiers used terror and torture to overcome the Chinese. As the fierce armies swept through China, hundreds of thousands of Chinese were taken prisoner. The Japanese felt the same hatred for the Chinese that the Nazis felt for the Jews, and the horrors that the Chinese people endured are nearly unimaginable.

"It may be pointless," one historian wrote, "to try to establish which World War II aggressor, Germany or Japan, was the more brutal to the peoples it victimized."

Mass murder, mass rape, use of poisonous gases, beheadings, burying people alive—the Japanese armies were consistently encouraged by their military leaders, as well as their emperor, Hirohito, to be as cruel as possible when dealing with the Chinese and their other enemies. Like the Nazis, they were also infamous for conducting "medical experiments" on their prisoners. For example, to try to find the best way to treat frostbite, they froze people's arms and legs and then chopped them off. In addition to all these horrors, germ warfare, a new and terrifying weapon, was introduced. Scholars estimate that as many as 748,000 Chinese people died from diseases like anthrax, bubonic plague, and cholera that were deliberately inflicted by the Japanese during the war.

Unlike Hitler, Emperor Hirohito was more inclined to follow the lead of his nation's military, rather than to impose a dictatorship. The military leaders as a group, however, felt very much like Hitler did. They believed that Japan's democratic government made it weak, and that allowing the people to vote and make their own decisions would eventually ruin Japan. The leaders warned that unless the Japanese devoted themselves 100 percent to their country and its military, Japan would never conquer China. Any Japanese who were not devoted were as good as dead.

"If there are any opposed to the 'Imperial Way' [Japan's takeover of other countries]," the Japanese war minister threatened, "we shall give them an injection with a bullet and bayonet."

Hitler was impressed by the Japanese and their military leaders. They would do anything to get the land they wanted. They were nationalistic. And they weren't afraid to be cruel and brutal. The Japanese were equally admiring of Hitler and his ways. Also, the Germans were in a war with the British, and the British owned some of the islands in the Pacific that Japan wanted. Perhaps, the Japanese military leaders thought, if they joined forces with Germany, they could have greater success. After all, Germany was no longer interested in the islands in the Pacific, and Japan was not interested in Europe.

For these reasons and more, Japan and Germany joined together. Italy's dictator, Mussolini, also saw the advantages of joining with Germany. Italy's army was neither strong nor particularly well-organized. Mussolini felt he would be protected by the Nazis, and, furthermore, he shared Hitler's views about dictatorship. By mid-1940, Japan, Italy, and Germany all signed an agreement to support one another and formed what became known as "the Axis."

Now the war was on; it was the Allies versus the Axis. Hitler was thrilled. Certainly, he thought, the Allies were no match for Germany and Japan. Perhaps the strongest countries of the Allies were Britain and France, but Hitler sneered at them.

"They are little worms," he scoffed.

The period of quiet and "sitzkrieg" in Europe

had passed. Even before the war in Poland ended, Hitler was planning how to best attack Britain. As though playing a giant board game, Hitler looked at the countries near England to figure out which move to make next. If he could control the North Sea, the body of water that separated Britain from northern Europe, the British navy wouldn't stand a chance. Norway and Denmark bordered the North Sea—they would be the Nazis' next victims of blitzkrieg.

On April 9, 1940, German soldiers swarmed Norway and Denmark as planes howled through the air, dropping bombs. Within hours, the terrified Danes surrendered to the Nazis without a fight. A day later, the king of Norway moved his country's government north, away from the German forces, but he eventually had to leave the country.

Prime Minister Chamberlain of Great Britain, who had believed that disputes with Hitler could be settled peacefully, now nervously sent troops to Norway. France sent troops, too. But the German forces were far more organized and well trained. Although the Allies fought bravely, they were outnumbered and were no match for the Germans. After about two months of fighting, the battle to save Norway ended in defeat for the Allied soldiers.

When news of the rapid successes reached Hitler, he wasted no time. Eyeing his map greedily, he knew which piece he wanted next: France. Hitler dreamed of walking through Paris—by the

Eiffel Tower, along the banks of the Seine River—knowing that it all belonged to him.

Now the Allies realized their terrible error. They had waited much too long to respond to Hitler. Many people in Britain were beginning to panic. "Hitler Cannot Be Stopped!" one newspaper headline announced. "Nazis on the Move!" shouted another. The Germans should never have been allowed to rebuild their military, the people protested. The finger of blame was pointed at Prime Minister Chamberlain. After all, wasn't he the one who had promised "peace for our time"? Hadn't he believed the lies Hitler had fed him and told the British people they had nothing to worry about?

Hitler's plan was now becoming frighteningly clear to everyone. He intended to take over Europe—and he was succeeding.

The outcry against Chamberlain became louder and louder. The British people demanded a stronger leader, someone who was tough and knew how to rally the British troops. Chamberlain knew it was time to step down and allow Britain to choose a new leader, and he didn't need to think twice about who that leader would be: Winston Churchill.

Churchill was well known in Britain. He had served as a brave and greatly admired commander of the British navy during World War I. However, after the war the Conservative government, which Churchill supported, became unpopular.

Conservatives favored keeping the military strong and ready to fight, but after the horror and death toll of World War I, most British people just wanted to forget about war. This is why, in part, when Hitler came along, most British people had initially supported Chamberlain. When Chamberlain said that he could just sit down and chat nicely with Hitler and avoid conflict, the British were all for it. Anything would be better than another war.

Churchill, on the other hand, had never agreed with Chamberlain. He had always seen Hitler as the dangerous and ruthless man that he was. While the rest of England seemed to be sleeping as Hitler made his plans, Churchill spoke out angrily. He thought it was shameful that the British had chosen to turn their backs on this growing threat rather than to meet it head-on.

"England has been offered a choice between war and shame," Churchill said in 1938. "She has chosen shame and will get war."

Many of the British ignored Churchill and labeled him "a loud-mouthed warmonger." Churchill had a very strong personality, a mischievous sense of humor, and an unusual talent for both writing and speaking. He refused to back down, and while, at the time, many British saw this as stubborn, it would be the exact personality needed to lead a country through wartime. Unlike Chamberlain, Churchill was never afraid to take risks. He was much less concerned with what the people of Britain thought of him than with responding quickly when the people of Britain were threatened.

As Hitler began taking over one country after another, the British people realized that Churchill had been right all along. Hitler's heavy footsteps grew closer, the thunder of the Nazi stormtroopers grew louder, and there was no denying that war was what England was going to get.

On May 10, 1940, Churchill was sworn in as the new prime minister of England. Now sixty-six years old, Churchill had been involved in politics and war debates for decades. He was a famous author and even a highly respected painter. He was the grandson of a duke and the son of a millionaire. He had traveled widely and dined with kings and queens. Surely, his appointment as prime minister was just the finishing touch to an amazing career.

However, Churchill saw it quite differently.

"I felt as if I were walking with destiny," he would later recall of that day, "and that all my past life had been but a preparation for this hour and for this trial."

And what a trial it would be. On the very afternoon of the day Churchill was sworn in, Hitler made his next move. Two countries practically on France's doorstep, Holland and Belgium, were attacked viciously with troops and bombing raids. Now, only France stood between Britain and the Nazis. A dread swept through England. How would England possibly survive the Nazi storm?

Would it not be better, some questioned aloud, to simply surrender before Britain was torn to pieces by Hitler?

In one of his first speeches as prime minister, Churchill gave a strong answer to those who questioned. In words so profound that the speech remains one of the most famous from World War II, Churchill proclaimed:

"Even though large tracts of Europe and many old and famous States have fallen or may fall into the grip of the Gestapo and . . . Nazi rule, we shall not flag or fail. We shall go on to the end, we shall fight in France, we shall fight on the seas and oceans, we shall fight with growing confidence and growing strength in the air, we shall defend our Island, whatever the cost may be, we shall fight on the beaches, we shall fight on the landing grounds, we shall fight in the fields and in the streets, we shall fight in the hills; we shall never surrender."

CHAPTER 5

Even before the war with Poland, Hitler had ordered the production of thousands of new bomber planes. There was nothing more terrifying, Hitler knew, than the sound of approaching bombers, the high-pitched shriek of bombs dropping, and the shattering explosion once they hit their targets. This was the sort of warfare Hitler planned to use on France and England. Belgium and Holland had surrendered in a matter of days, being no match at all for the German war machine. Hitler assumed France and England would surrender, too—it would simply take a bit more firepower.

When Germany struck northern France in mid-May 1940, the French were taken completely by surprise. In an area known as the Ardennes Forest, huge German tanks, called "panzers," suddenly came roaring through the thick woods. It was as if they had appeared out of nowhere. The French had thought the forests were much too dense and the few forest roads much too narrow for the German military to pass through. But the French were wrong. Within days, 10,000 French soldiers were captured. Some were so terrified of the Germans that they simply threw down their weapons and put their hands up in surrender as soon as they saw the panzers break through the forests.

Meanwhile, British forces sent to help defend the French were not doing much better. The German troops had managed to successfully trap several hundred thousand soldiers, both French and British, on the beach at Dunkirk on the northern coast of France. The Germans had done this by closing in from all sides until the Allies had nowhere to turn but the English Channel, the body of water separating France and England. With no boats or other means to escape, it looked as though the Allies were going to be massacred by the Nazi troops. Back in Britain, Churchill paced nervously.

"It is a colossal military disaster!" he roared in frustration. The first major battle effort by the British looked as though it was going to be both an embarrassment and a slaughter.

German dive bombers roared over the beach at Dunkirk. Desperate soldiers, with nowhere to hide, huddled on the ground with their hands over their heads. Some of the bravest stood up and shot their rifles into the air at the bombers. Of course, these shots did no good—and the soldiers could see no way out of their desperate predicament.

Then, surprisingly, the German armies stopped their advance. Perhaps the troops needed to rest or maintain their equipment, or perhaps the commanders thought there was no rush, since their enemy was hopelessly trapped.

As night fell and the bombers retreated, the Allied soldiers watched in disbelief as small boats, one after another, came quietly to the shores of Dunkirk. Tattered fishing boats, family sailboats, a passenger ferry, and even rowboats lined up to rescue the soldiers. The British Royal Navy had sent out the word to all those who lived across the channel in England, begging for assistance. On May 26, 1940, the first night of what came to be known as "the rescue by the little ships of Dunkirk," more than 7,000 soldiers were ferried back to England. The next night, nearly 18,000 men quietly crept aboard the rescue vessels. By the time the operation ended ten days later, 340,000 Allied troops—both British and French—had been taken safely to England. People cheered in the streets, and the newspapers proclaimed the rescue a miracle.

However, Churchill, always one for keeping a realistic outlook, was not so quick to celebrate. "Wars are not won by evacuations," he warned matter-of-factly.

In his mind, this had been a remarkable event, but it had certainly not been a victory. After all, the German troops had sent the Allies scurrying home to safety. Still, the willingness of the British people—from high-ranking military officials to poor fishermen—to work together was a huge inspiration. It was this kind of spirit that would pull the British through some very difficult days.

And now those hard times were just around the corner. The German troops had been getting closer and closer to Paris, and it was all too clear that Hitler intended to crush the city to dust if he had to. The French government made the difficult decision to surrender to the Nazis so that they would not destroy Paris, one of the most beautiful cities in the world. Although they would be giving up, defeat was already certain, and the French agreed that it would be better to let Hitler have his way than to watch Paris burn to the ground. The agreement between France and Germany was signed on June 22, 1940.

Yet it wasn't enough for Hitler to have control of France—he wanted to humiliate the French. He insisted on having the French sign their surrender in the very same railway car where the Germans had signed their surrender following World War I. Following this bit of spitefulness, Hitler and his commanders strolled through Paris, snapping pictures of one another and posing proudly in front of the Eiffel Tower.

Making matters worse for the French, Italy's dictator, Mussolini, decided to invade southern France and grab some land while France was weak and defeated. Hitler, who was not particularly concerned about the south of France, gave Mussolini permission to take what he wanted. Unlike the

Germans, however, the Italian people and their military did not support their leader wholeheartedly. Many saw Mussolini as a cruel, selfish man with no real plan other than to follow behind Hitler and take the leftovers of war. Nonetheless, this attack on France marked Italy's formal entry into World War II as one of the Axis powers.

It was now late summer of 1940, and Adolf Hitler's dream was rapidly coming true—more rapidly than even he had imagined. In only one year of fighting, the Nazis had gained control of nearly all of Europe. Britain now stood alone against the dreaded German military. Hermann Goering, the commander of the German air force, scorned the idea that the British would be able or willing to put up any kind of real fight.

"My *Luftwaffe* [air force] is invincible," Goering announced. "And so now we turn to England. How long will this one last—two, three weeks?"

Although the British had been slow to respond to the Nazi threat, they had agreed to take in Jewish children from Germany and Poland in the years leading up to the war. Perhaps Chamberlain had not been very clear-sighted about Hitler, but he was not blind to how cruelly Jewish people were being treated by the Nazis. The British may not have known about the murders in the woods or the starvation and beatings in the prison camps, but they knew that Jewish mothers and fathers feared desperately for the futures of their children. When the news of Kristallnacht reached England, the British knew that they needed to take quick action to save the children.

Special rescue trains known as *"Kindertransports,* or "child transports," began moving Jewish children from eastern European countries to safety in England. About 10,000 children found themselves hurriedly hugging their parents goodbye at train stations. The very youngest were infants who would remember nothing of this separation. And young children often thought they were going on a fun trip with a lot of other people their age. The older children, some as old as 16, however, were often confused or frightened.

"I got the notion into my head that my parents wanted to get rid of me," a Kindertransport child named Hedy Epstein recalled many years later. "My parents were trying to paint a wonderful picture for me of England. . . . It must have been very painful for them."

As Hedy's parents pinned a large number on her so that her new family in England could identify her when she stepped off the train, they reassured her that this was only temporary and that her time in England would fly by. But Hedy, at 14 years old, could recognize that her parents' smiles were artificial. Hedy followed the other children into the passenger cars and took a seat by the window. Outside, parents were waving, and all of them,

Hedy couldn't help but notice, were wearing the same phony smiles.

As the train's engine began warming up, Hedy's mother and father came over and tapped on her window.

"Don't forget to say 'thank you' and 'please'!" her mother shouted through the glass.

Then the train began to move. In a single fluid movement, all the parents began to follow the train, slowly at first, and then running as the train picked up speed. All the parents were still waving, but now Hedy could see that her mother's smile had disappeared. She had never seen her father cry before, but now tears streamed down his face as he ran beside her window.

"Then I knew: They really *did* love me," Hedy remembered. "This was a great act of love. I watched them getting smaller and smaller until they were two dots, and then they were gone."

Like nearly all of the other Kindertransport children, Hedy would never see her parents again. Not long after she boarded that rescue train heading west, her parents would be forced onto a very different kind of train—a train headed east to the concentration camps in Poland.

For a while the Nazis did not interfere with the Kindertransports. After all, they wanted to get rid of Jews, particularly children and the elderly. If Jews could find a way to send their children elsewhere, it would save the Nazis the trouble of dealing with the "problem." However, once the war broke out and Hitler continued to take over big sections of Europe, he ordered the Kindertransports stopped. He intended to conquer England, too, and he didn't want thousands of Jewish children in England any more than he wanted them in Germany.

By late 1939, Hitler told his armies to shoot any children caught trying to leave Germany or Poland for England. One of the last transports, a secret one in 1940, was caught by the Gestapo, which marched many of the children into the woods to meet a grisly death. Since the children all carried identification, many of the parents were also tracked down and killed.

Once the transports were stopped, the future looked very grim for Jewish children. Aside from hiding, there was no hope for them to find safety. Even those in hiding often died from starvation and disease. By 1945, the Nazis would have murdered more than 1.5 million children, most of them Jewish. However, when World War II finally ended, nearly all of the 10,000 Kindertransport children had survived. As a result, they became known as "the children who escaped Hitler."

Now, as war loomed for the British people, the parents of children who lived in London felt the same panic that parents on the European mainland had felt. London would be the target of the Nazis, and it would be an exceedingly dangerous place for a child to be. Once again, thousands of children were put on trains and sent out to the countryside to live. If they were lucky, they went to the homes of relatives, but many were sent to spend the next four years with strangers. Sometimes parents accompanied their children, but more often than not, the parents stayed behind, waving tearful farewells at the London train station.

"A war is such a terrible thing," said one young mother who sent her daughter to live with relatives where Jewish children were already living. "It shouldn't involve children—they are innocent. They are the utter opposite of everything that war is about."

Hitler and his forces were now busily planning their attack on Britain. It was to be the blitz of all blitzes, a tremendous display of terror and firepower, courtesy of the much-dreaded German air force, the Luftwaffe. Hitler intended to create a kind of misery and fear that, he believed, would break the spirit of the British people. A broken spirit, Hitler believed, was the next best thing to death.

And far away, on the other side of Europe, the process of destroying Jews by attempting to break their spirit was well under way. By 1940, hundreds of Jewish ghettos had been established in Poland, Romania, Hungary, and beyond. The purpose of the ghettos had now taken a grim turn. At first, they had simply been a way for the Nazis to control the Jews and keep them gathered in one place. In addition, when Jews were forced out of their homes at gunpoint in the middle of the night, they had to leave everything behind. This created incredible wealth for the Nazis, who literally piled silver, jewelry, and precious artwork on street corners for trucks to collect.

But now, more and more frequently, the ghettos were becoming holding centers. If Hitler had once considered allowing Jews to remain indefinitely in these crammed, filthy corners of cities throughout Eastern Europe, he had now changed his mind. Briefly, he had considered shipping all European Jews to a distant and dry part of Africa, but when Hitler realized how expensive this would be, he changed his plan. The new plan was to systematically collect Jews into ghettos and then, just as systematically, transport them—*all* of them—to concentration camps. There, they would be worked, beaten, or starved to death.

Of course, it didn't take long for Hitler to realize that the Nazis' work could be cut in half if the Jews did not have to be transported and resettled in the camps. Perhaps if life could be made as miserable as possible in the ghettos, Hitler thought, a large portion of Jews would die there first.

"I do not see why man should not be just as cruel as nature," Hitler said angrily when questioned about his increasingly brutal plans for the Jews. After all, Hitler believed, Jews were weak and unfit to live. In nature, it was survival of the fittest. From flowers to insects to elephants, only the strong survived—there was no pity for weakness. Strength was necessary for a species to continue. And now Hitler believed he was doing his part, God's will, to ensure the continuation of flawless human beings.

So the ghettos became little corners of hell. They were several-block worlds of filth, barbed wire, and constant terror. In some ghettos, food rations were reduced to 200 calories (about one piece of bread) per person per day. Running water was cut off, and many people became so desperate for water that they drank their own urine. Deadly diseases claimed so many lives that corpses were piled fifteen deep in some ghetto streets.

Hitler's Gestapo chiefs returned to him from the ghettos with reports of the horror, and Hitler was pleased.

"The earth continues to go round, whether it's the man who kills the tiger or the tiger who eats the man," Hitler pointed out proudly. "The stronger asserts his will; it's the law of nature. The world doesn't change; its laws are eternal."

CHAPTER 6

When one reads about these endless cruelties the Nazis committed against the Jews, the first question often is "Why didn't the Jews fight back?" It seems unbelievable that millions of people would simply walk quietly and obediently to their deaths.

They didn't.

The idea that no Jewish people ever fought back against Nazi control is a myth. Jews often fought against the Nazis—in nearly every ghetto and even in the concentration camps. What is not a myth, however, is that very little of what the Jews did had any real or lasting impact on the German military.

A number of factors contributed to the Jews' reluctance or inability to fight back. In general, Jewish people preferred to settle their disputes peacefully. They tried to avoid fighting and prayed that solutions could instead be found through compromise. Furthermore, many Jews did not believe that the Nazi government was really as dangerous as many people said it was. Historically, German Jews had always been very proud of their country and its people. They couldn't imagine that their own country would intentionally harm them.

And while Jews were not happy with how they were being treated, many continued to believe that they really *were* going to be resettled in a different part of Europe before long, and that the nightmare of ghettos, trigger-happy soldiers, and hunger would be over. After all, even today it is difficult to grasp a plan as evil as Hitler's. How much more difficult it must have been for the Jews to imagine or believe it during that time.

Additionally, by the time many Jews began to realize what was happening to them, most were weak with hunger and sickness. All were without any kind of weapons. And it had become all too clear that the result of any kind of resistance was a rifle to one's head. The choice was plain: Follow the Nazis' rules and maybe live to see another day, or fight back and get shot. As one Jewish man who struggled in the Warsaw Ghetto explained, "It is very difficult to raise even a finger against a machine gun." And so, many Jews, terrified and broken, did not resist.

However, many other Jews did.

Elie Wiesel, a former concentration camp prisoner who later wrote about his experiences, once said, "The question is not why all the Jews did *not* fight, but how so many of them *did*. Tormented, beaten, starved, where did they find the strength—spiritual and physical—to resist?"

As Wiesel indicated, resistance did not necessarily involve a plan to physically attack guards or fight back with fists and violence. Resistance could come instead from the spirit. Jews who refused to let Hitler and the Nazis break their spirit or crush their hope won important personal battles. Although the Nazis did everything they could to make the Jews feel as though they were worthless and less than human, many Jews found ways to maintain their dignity.

Within the ghettos, this was not easy. Starvation was one of the main tools the Nazis used to turn humans into animals. They discovered that if people were hungry enough, they would stoop to the lowest depths just to obtain a stale crust of bread. The Nazi guards enjoyed standing outside the gates of the ghettos or along the tall stone walls and making a game of throwing leftovers from their lunches into crowds of desperate children. Sometimes the guards would laugh as the children fought viciously, tearing hair and drawing blood for just an apple core. Other times, the guards would toss food toward the children and then shoot at them as they scurried toward it.

A young boy named Roman Halter, who lived in a Polish ghetto, remembered how the lack of food was often dehumanizing. He had friends who, because they were children, were small enough to lower themselves into the sewers and trudge through the underground tunnels that led out of the ghettos. Sometimes the children would slog through nearly a mile of garbage and human waste in order to beg on the streets outside the ghetto. The begging was dangerous. If the children were discovered to be Jews who had escaped the ghetto, they were likely to be beaten or killed. But death was death, whether from lack of food or from a rifle. Many children, and even adults, were willing to take the chances that seemed necessary to save their lives.

Roman was starving just like everyone else around him. But he recalled an elderly couple's example of dignity. It was a memory that stuck with him during his most difficult times. Roman and his family lived in a cramped room along with several other people. As with food, there was never enough space either. It was not uncommon for a dozen people to occupy a room barely big enough for four people.

One day, an older couple joined the already over-crowded space. Roman noticed an odd habit that the two old people shared. Every evening, Roman would stand in the long lines near the ghetto's center waiting for dinner. In reality, "dinner" was nothing more than a small bowl of thin broth with a piece of potato floating around in it. But as soon as he grabbed his bowl, Roman wolfed down the food like a wild animal. Everyone else did the same thing—everyone except the elderly couple.

Roman watched them slowly climb the stairs with their bowls balanced carefully. Once they reached the small room, they set their bowls on a battered table, said a blessing, and placed napkins in their laps. Then they drank the liquid of the soup while chatting about their day as if they had not a care in the world. Then, with fork and knife, they delicately cut up the morsels of potato and ate them slowly as though they were enjoying a steak.

To Roman, this seemed ridiculous. Finally, he asked the old man why they did it.

"If you lose your self-dignity," the man explained to the boy, "then you are lost. Then you really become what they want you to become."

Roman realized that, in their small way, this couple was resisting the Nazi oppression by remaining the people they had always been.

The Nazis not only starved the Jews' bodies with lack of food in the ghettos. They also attempted to starve the Jews' brains and souls by taking away all kinds of mental stimulation. They murdered some of the brightest and most talented people in Jewish communities. They burned books and newspapers, banned religious ceremonies, and strictly prohibited schools. The Nazis believed that education was wasted on a Jewish child. If a child was old enough to go to school, he or she was old enough to work.

Alicia Appleman was ten years old when her family was forced into a ghetto. She was assigned cleaning jobs outside of the ghetto, mostly polishing the silver and fine furniture that the Nazis had taken from Jewish families. Once, as she began cleaning a nightstand, she realized that it had belonged to her own father. Just a month earlier, Alicia's father had been taken to the woods and shot by the Nazis only because he was a well educated man and a leading citizen of the Jewish community. Tears blurred Alicia's eyes as she continued her work, but the determination in her soul was stronger than her sorrow. She would not let the Nazis break her spirit, she told herself.

A week later, Alicia was told to scrub the floors at an elementary school—her old school. Students and former friends gawked at the Jewish girl in tattered clothes, wearing the Star of David armband. The armband, a yellow star, let everyone know that the wearer was Jewish. It was against the law for any Jewish person to remove the armband. To do so could mean death. Even so, after all the students had left for another class, Alicia took off her armband and walked around her old classroom just so she could imagine she was still a student there. It seemed to give her a sense, if only briefly, of hope and personal strength.

Then later that day, as Alicia was leaving to head back to the ghetto, she could hear her favorite teacher's voice coming through an open window on the second floor of the school. Before she knew it, she was doing something quite dangerous and certainly forbidden.

"The desire to learn overcame the warnings I had received about staying away," Alicia later wrote.

Alicia was so hungry for learning that she climbed a tree outside the classroom and stared through the window at her classmates. She became so interested in the lesson being taught that she completely forgot that she was hanging onto a tree limb. And when her teacher asked the class a question, Alicia eagerly raised her hand to offer an answer.

Wham!

Alicia fell out of the tree, drawing the attention of the classroom and the teacher. Luckily, her teacher, like many Christian Polish and German people, did not agree with what the Nazis were doing and did not report Alicia. Instead, she rushed out to make sure her former student was not hurt and then helped her to her feet.

"Alicia, you know you can't do this," the teacher whispered, brushing her off.

"But I don't mind the tree," Alicia responded sadly, hoping she could continue to secretly learn in this way.

"It is too dangerous," the teacher said, gently touching Alicia's Star of David band. "Do you understand?"

Alicia nodded. She understood the danger clearly, but she understood the far greater danger of giving in to the Nazis even more clearly. She would never give up and let fear crush her. It was this fighting spirit that, in the end, would save Alicia Appleman's life after years of hiding, running, standing up to Nazis, and refusing to back down.

Thousands of other Jews trapped in the ghettos fought secretly in their own ways. Adults worked to smuggle in paper and watercolors so that children could paint pictures of their happiest memories. Teachers gathered children in hidden rooms and taught them, in whispers, how to read and write. Songs were written, holy days were celebrated, and young people even danced in the streets when the Nazi guards weren't watching. Many guards were angry when they caught Jews involved in such illegal activities. But just as many guards scratched their heads in wonder. How, in the midst of misery and death, could these people continue to celebrate life?

And some Jews fought back with fists and guns, too. Perhaps the most famous resistance took place in the Warsaw Ghetto in Poland. This was the largest ghetto of all, with nearly half a million Jews jammed into barely 1.3 square miles of space. It was terribly overcrowded, but it was better than the alternative: being sent to a concentration camp.

In 1943, the Nazis were in the process of clearing out, or "liquidating," the ghettos by sending every single Jew to the camps. By mid-April, around 70,000 Jews remained in the Warsaw Ghetto. Among them were up to 1,000 "ghetto fighters," who called themselves the Jewish Combat Organization. They were determined to fight to the finish and not go quietly to the camps. With smuggled guns and homemade bombs and grenades, these Jews fired on the approaching

Nazis. Their attack was so successful that the Nazis turned around in a panic and ran.

When Hitler received word of this uprising, he was furious. How was it that more than 2,000 Germans, well armed with machine guns, rifles, tanks, and flamethrowers, could not defeat a poorly armed force half their size? Right away, Hitler fired the general in charge of the Warsaw Ghetto and instructed a new general to crush the revolt immediately. Hitler laughed at the idea of Jews having the nerve to put up much of a fight. He was certain that the Warsaw Ghetto would be liquidated within three days.

However, three days, six days, twelve days, and more went by. The revolt showed no sign of weakening. The Jewish fighters barricaded themselves in buildings and courtyards, and shot sniperlike through windows and dark doorways. Several armored German tanks were even set on fire by carefully aimed grenades. Finally, Hitler had had enough.

"Burn the ghetto to the ground!" he bellowed. "Trap them in there and burn them alive."

Surrounded by ten-foot stone walls and barbed wire, the ghetto fighters had no way out as the flames grew higher. Eyewitnesses reported seeing dozens of people on fire screaming and jumping out of windows to their death.

"The sea of flames flooded houses and court-yards," one resistance leader remembered. "There was no air, only black, choking smoke and heavy burning heat radiating from the red-hot walls, from the glowing stone stairs."

Still, the Jews refused to surrender. Some tried to escape through sewer tunnels, but the Nazis caught on and flooded the sewers. Some tried to hide behind the burned-out rubble, but the Nazis sent in their police dogs to sniff them out. In the end, of the 56,000 Jews captured, 7,000 were shot on the spot, and the rest were sent to the camps.

"We were beaten by the flames, not the Germans," one of the ghetto fighters remarked bitterly, refusing to give credit to the Nazis for ultimately crushing the uprising.

The Warsaw uprising had shaken the Nazis and given a glimmer of hope to the Jews. No one, particularly not Hitler, had ever expected the Jews to fight back so bravely and, for a short time, successfully. Finally, on May 16, 1943, twenty-seven days after the ghetto fighters had fired their first shots, the new general breathed a sigh of relief and wrote to the Führer: "The ghetto is no more."

In the summer of 1940, however, the resistance of Jews was of little concern to Hitler. He had his eye on the ultimate prize: England. Hitler's plan was simple enough. He would have his air force commander, Hermann Goering, lead the Luftwaffe in an air raid unlike anything the world had ever seen. Goering had continued to brag that the Luftwaffe could shut down the Royal Air Force (or "RAF," as England's air force was called) in only a few days.

In fact, Hitler did not believe that England had either the will or the finances to continue fighting for very long.

"England, unlike in 1914, will not allow herself to blunder into a war lasting for years," Hitler predicted. "Such is the fate of rich countries. . . . Not even England has the money nowadays to fight a world war."

And so Hitler looked at his maps again. Once the Luftwaffe had destroyed the RAF, it would be simple enough for many thousands of German troops to cross the narrow English Channel from France. With no fear of an air attack, the Nazis could storm through England and force the British to their knees.

"And who will come to the aid of Britain *now*?" Hitler asked his commanders with a cruel grin. England had far-flung allies in Australia, Canada, and India, but they would be of no help. England was now an island, both literally and symbolically. She stood alone.

As the day of the blitz grew closer, Hitler rallied the German troops. This was it! Once England fell, the Nazis would control all of Europe. The attack must be quick, brutal, and without mercy. Hitler raised his fists and shook them at the heavens. His eyes blazed, and he shouted his command to the sea of saluting soldiers.

"A single blow must destroy the enemy . . . without regard of losses . . . a gigantic all-destroying blow."

CHAPTER 7

"**T**here's one coming down in flames—there, somebody's hit a German and he's coming down. There's a long streak—he's coming down completely out of control . . . a long streak of smoke. The pilot's bailed out by parachute—he was in a Junkers 87 dive bomber and he's going slap into the sea and there he goes—smash! Oh boy, I've never seen anything so good as this. . . . The RAF fighters have really got these boys . . . !"

A radio reporter for the British Broadcasting Corporation excitedly watched an air fight over the English Channel on July 14, 1940, and reported it blow by blow. As frightening as it was, many British were thrilled by the air shows of these dueling fighter planes. This was the first all-air battle in the entire history of war, so it was truly something remarkable to watch.

Unlike the bomber planes, the fighters were not particularly dangerous to civilians. They were designed to shoot down other planes, not to attack land targets. As a result, the first phase of Germany's attack on England became something of a game for the British to watch from the sidelines and cheer on.

A ten-year-old boy, bored in his Sunday school class, recalled the sound of zooming fighters getting louder and louder until his teacher could no longer be heard over their roar. At that point, everyone, adults and children alike, rushed out of the church and stared skyward.

"Everyone was excited rather than frightened, and there being no air raid shelter, we thought it safer to be outside rather than inside," the boy recalled. "So we all lay on the churchyard grass and had a thrilling view of the twists and turns of those marvelous men in their flying machines engaged in single combat above us."

The Germans had been building new planes nonstop leading up to the attack, and now the planes in the Luftwaffe outnumbered those in the RAF by 2,500 to 1,200. Even so, the British clearly maintained the upper hand. For one thing, the British had developed a new technology before the war had even begun: radar. While the Germans had to send in fighter after fighter to track down the RAF planes, the British were able to trace the paths of the incoming fighters and intercept them. This was both frustrating and baffling to the Germans.

Making matters worse for the Luftwaffe, their targets were a long way from their airfields. German planes took off from occupied areas of France, but by the time the fighters got to England and flew one patrol, they had to return to France for fuel. They simply could not carry enough fuel to fight effectively. And perhaps most important, the British pilots were unexpectedly (to the Germans, anyway) brave and talented. At the end of the first phase of the Battle of Britain, the Luftwaffe had lost about 600 planes compared with about 300 lost by the RAF.

"Never in the field of human conflict was so much owed by so many to so few," Winston Churchill said, noting that even though the RAF had been terribly outnumbered, it had been successful.

Commander Goering was embarrassed; Adolf Hitler was enraged.

"It is time to change tactics," Goering announced grimly.

It was time for the second phase of the Battle of Britain, the phase that would become known simply as "the Blitz." Now, the focus was on bombing—both airfields and cities. London, in particular, was attacked viciously. Raid after raid dropped bombs right in the most heavily populated sections of the city. Londoners were not prepared for such an attack and had only one place to hide safely: the city's subway, known as "the Tube." Thousands of people crammed into the dark tunnels for hours as the earth shook with bomb strikes. Makeshift beds, complete with sheets and blankets, were lined up end to end through the subway tunnels in an effort to make children feel more comfortable. However, as one British child bluntly noted, "The beds was nice, but we was still in the Tube."

The Blitz was devastating. More than 43,000 civilians were killed, 140,000 were injured, and 20 percent of London's buildings were turned to ashes and rubble. From his experience, Hitler knew what happens when a country is so badly beaten up: It gives up. People lose hope, and then they lose the will to fight.

But not this time. The worse things got, the more determined the British became. They were not satisfied with just holding on against the Germans; they wanted to beat them. "London can take it!" became the slogan, and even after the worst bombings, people chanted it in the streets. The RAF continued to fight back courageously, and stood up to every attack by the Luftwaffe, destroying more and more bombers with every strike. Churchill rallied his nation:

"Hitler knows that he will have to break us in this Island or lose the war. If we can stand up to him, all Europe may be free. . . . But if we fail, then the whole world . . . will sink into the abyss of a new Dark Age. . . . Let us therefore brace ourselves to our duties, and so bear ourselves that, if the British Empire and the Commonwealth last for a thousand years, men will still say, 'This was their finest hour.'"

Hitler grew increasingly frustrated. Why didn't the British surrender? No amount of bombs or threats seemed to make them back down. Finally,

Hitler decided to focus elsewhere. He had bloodied England, and that was good enough for the time being. He would continue air raids on the British, but now Hitler wanted a new challenge. First, however, he had to come to the rescue of a blundering Italian army.

Mussolini had desperately wanted to show the world that he was just as powerful and fierce as Hitler was. In many ways, however, he was completely at odds with what Hitler was trying to do. While Hitler was attempting to take over all of Europe, Mussolini continued to brag about building "a new Roman Empire." And while Hitler's armies were highly trained and devoted to their battles, Mussolini's military was a disaster. Mussolini had attempted to conquer Egypt in North Africa, only to have his tanks run out of fuel. Next, he went after Greece and lost half his battleships and was kicked out of the country.

The British had come to the aid of Greece and Egypt, so Hitler felt obliged to come to the aid of Italy. In barely ten days, the Nazis overtook Greece, despite the presence of 60,000 British troops. It was one of Hitler's most stunning victories, and it gave him such overwhelming confidence that he truly believed he and his Nazis were unstoppable.

With his ego in overdrive, Hitler began looking for bigger challenges. Why not go after the world's largest country? In 1939, Hitler had promised the Soviet Union's leader, Joseph Stalin, that he would leave the Soviet Union alone. But Hitler was not one to keep promises. He hated Communism, the Soviets' form of government, and he placed all Communists barely a step above Jews. In addition, much to Hitler's disgust, there were several million Jews in the Soviet Union.

Nonetheless, the Soviet Union was rich in resources, and it would provide endless "living space" for Hitler's master race. He eyed the country greedily. It would be easy to overtake, Hitler believed. The people were poor, and many of them disliked Stalin, who was a heavy-handed and often cruel leader. Surely, Hitler thought, people who do not support their leader will not put up much of a fight for their country.

"We have only to kick in the door," Hitler said of attacking the Soviet Union, "and the whole rotten structure will come crashing down."

Hitler's ego had finally clouded his sharp, if cruel, mind. His long downward spiral was about to begin.

The Soviet Union's military was not much more advanced than Poland's had been when that country was attacked in 1939. Stalin simply refused to believe that Hitler was actually going to attack the Soviet Union. Stalin repeatedly told his army generals that they had nothing to worry about. After all, hadn't he and Hitler signed a "non-aggression" pact? Then on June 22, 1941, the Germans began firing on Soviet soldiers. One confused soldier sent a panicked message to headquarters saying, "We are being fired upon. What shall we do?"

The general in charge, believing what Stalin had always told him, simply responded, "You must be crazy."

All things considered, it did seem as though the Soviet Union's defense *was* a "rotten structure," but there were two important things that Hitler hadn't counted on: the toughness of the Soviet people and the bitterness of the Soviet winter.

"In spite of the distances we were advancing," wrote one German soldier of the Nazis' invasion of the Soviet Union, "there was no feeling, as there had been in France, of entry into a defeated nation. Instead there was resistance, always resistance, however hopeless."

Everyone fought—soldiers, farmers, women, and even children. Women strapped rifles and swords onto their backs and joined the guerilla forces. Children threw rocks and garbage at the Germans as they marched through villages. Perhaps many of the Soviets did not like Stalin, but they loved their homeland. Millions of Soviets were slaughtered, yet they fought on bravely. Because the Soviet Union was such a large country, there were always millions more who were willing to sacrifice their lives.

Back in Berlin, Hitler paced angrily. "The Soviets fight with a truly stupid fanaticism," he scoffed, refusing to admit that these "subhumans" were often more courageous than his own soldiers.

With the winter of 1941 upon them, the Germans realized that they had underestimated just how brutal a Soviet winter could be. At temperatures of 50 degrees below zero, machine guns wouldn't fire, tanks wouldn't start up, and soldiers could barely move. Far from home and running out of supplies, many troops soon found themselves without even enough fuel to start a fire. As soldiers froze to death, rats moved in to eat their remains. And, in turn, the rats spread disease among the living soldiers.

Finally, Hitler commanded the German troops to return to their camps and remain there until spring. They could rest, and prepare to fight again in several months. It was December, only weeks before Christmas. The British, though still not backing down, were, in Hitler's opinion, under control. The Nazis had conquered most of the rest of Europe. It was the perfect time to take a break, Hitler thought. It was December 6, 1941.

The very next morning, thousands of miles away, 183 Japanese bomber and fighter planes took off from a line of aircraft carriers steaming through the Pacific Ocean about 230 miles north of the Hawaiian Islands. They flew above a thick cloud cover. Some of the Japanese pilots worried that the clouds would block their view when they reached their target. But then, just as the planes neared the target, the clouds parted. The pilots felt that this was a sign of approval from a higher power.

Beneath the planes was the city of Honolulu. And just west of that city, in the southern part of the island, was the destination of all 183 planes: Pearl Harbor. Pearl Harbor was the headquarters of the United States Pacific Fleet. Eight battleships lined the harbor, fighter planes waited on seven nearby airfields, and thousands of soldiers were stationed at the base. But it was a sleepy Sunday morning, and there had not been even a whisper of warning of what was approaching. Most of the American soldiers were still in their bunks.

Suddenly, the thunder of exploding bombs and gunfire filled the island air. Shrill alarms shrieked, and the announcement "Air raid, Pearl Harbor! This is not a drill!" was repeated urgently. Japan had hoped to surprise the Americans, and their plan had worked perfectly. Before American troops could even put their boots and helmets on, 90 percent of all the damage at Pearl Harbor had been done. Twelve warships were sunk or damaged, 188 planes were destroyed, and about 2,400 Americans were killed. On one battleship alone, the *Arizona*, over 1,000 men were killed when a bomb, in a one-in-a-million chance, fell through the deck into the ammunition storage area of the ship. It exploded in a blinding flash of light, blowing sailors to bits and setting the very water on fire with gasoline and debris.

The Japanese had planned a second and even third wave of attack, but the American soldiers had manned their anti-aircraft guns by that time, and the Japanese had much less success. The damage had been done, however. It had taken only one and a half hours for the U.S. Pacific Fleet to be badly crippled.

Why had the Japanese attacked the United States? What in the world did the United States have to do with Japan's quest for more land? Essentially, the United States was simply in the way. For some time, Japan had been eyeing quite a few islands and areas of rich natural resources in the South Pacific, and many of those areas were protected by the United States' forces based at Pearl Harbor. Japanese military leaders looked at a number of different options and finally decided to take a gamble. If they could catch the United States completely off-guard and seriously damage its Pacific fleet, they stood a good chance of being able to rush in and grab land while the United States was still reeling in shock.

At first, the Pearl Harbor attack looked like a terrific success. Japan's prime minister, Hideki Tojo, celebrated and praised the Japanese military for its wise move. But Admiral Isoroku Yamamoto, who had planned the strike, was not so quick to pat himself on the back. Yamamoto had lived in the United States for several years. He had studied at Harvard University and had visited the U.S. Naval War College in Rhode Island. He understood

Americans quite well—certainly better than the Japanese prime minister did.

Yamamoto had warned Tojo that the United States was a mighty force and not one to be taken lightly. Furthermore, bombing Pearl Harbor in a surprise attack had seemed cowardly and wrong to Yamamoto. He had agreed to it reluctantly.

"A military man can scarcely pride himself on having smitten a sleeping enemy," Yamamoto said carefully after the attack. "It is more a matter of shame, simply, for the one smitten."

Shameful or not, it created an immediate and worldwide chain reaction. America declared war on Japan. And the two other members of the Axis, Germany and Italy, came to Japan's defense and declared war on the United States. Just as instantly, Britain promised to fight on the side of the United States. From the cold, barren plains of the Soviet Union to London to New York City and on to the tropical islands of the Pacific and the misty mountains of Japan, the entire world was now at war.

Yamamoto took a deep breath and shook his head in worry. When asked why he did not believe the attack on United States' base had been a success, Yamamoto replied, "I fear all we have done is to awaken a sleeping giant and fill him with a terrible resolve."

CHAPTER 8

"**Y**esterday, December 7, 1941—a date which will live in infamy—the United States of America was suddenly and deliberately attacked by naval and air forces of the Empire of Japan."

President Franklin Delano Roosevelt addressed a rare joint session of the U.S. Congress the day after the attack on Pearl Harbor. Roosevelt did not try to avoid the facts or make things look better than they were—that was not his style. He was a straightforward, tough President who did not flinch when telling the American people what to expect.

"There is no blinking at the fact that our people, our territory, and our interests are in grave danger," Roosevelt continued. "With confidence in our armed forces, with the unbounding determination of our people, we will gain the inevitable triumph. So help us God."

The United States was now headed into the war, but for quite some time it had tried very hard to stay out of all the brewing conflicts across the oceans. After World War I, many Americans had felt that getting involved in a "European war" had been a mistake. Over 100,000 Americans had died in that war, and some Americans bitterly argued that the United States should never have gotten dragged into World War I in the first place.

As a result, in the 1920s and 1930s the United States began following a foreign policy of isolationism. The country decided to remain as far away from the rest of the world's problems as possible. It avoided becoming involved in the conflicts in Europe or Asia and remained neutral about wars in any other parts of the world. The United States believed, mistakenly, that it didn't need allies—that it could handle things on its own.

When Roosevelt became President in 1933, the United States was in the midst of the Great Depression, so most of Roosevelt's energy was focused on trying to rebuild the economy. Certainly, Americans were not blind to what Hitler was doing in Europe, but like the President, they were more concerned about how the country was going to dig itself out of a depression. During this time, a number of laws were passed called "neutrality laws." These laws assured that the United States would stay out of everyone else's war business and would take care of itself.

Then when France fell to the Germans, Americans got nervous. It was beginning to look like Hitler was pretty serious. What if the Nazis really *did* take over England? Wouldn't that put the

United States in a lot of danger? How would the United States survive if Germany tried to overtake it, too—especially if countries that had been allies of the United States were already under German control? A lot of Americans began to think that being isolated and neutral might not be the best idea.

That idea occurred to Roosevelt, too. He began to look for ways around the neutrality laws so that the United States could help the British as they continued to fight the Germans.

"If your neighbor's house caught fire and he had no garden hose," Roosevelt said as a way of explaining to the American people why the country should help England, "the prudent thing to do in order to prevent the fire from spreading is to lend him your hose."

So to help control the wildfire of German aggression, the United States sent war materials to Britain to help it build more warships. And when the Germans began sinking more British warships than the British could replace, the United States sent fleets of its own ships. These were supposed to be used only as patrol ships, not as active warships, but the Germans didn't believe that would happen. In late 1941, German U-boats ("underwater boats," or submarines) began firing on American ships. In one incident, more than 100 U.S. sailors were killed.

Americans, now, were even more nervous.

"I have said this before," Roosevelt assured Americans, "but I shall say it again and again: Your boys are not going to be sent into any foreign wars."

In a sense, the Germans had *already* drawn the United States into a "foreign war." However, when Japan bombed Pearl Harbor only six weeks later, Roosevelt was able to keep his promise. It was no longer some overseas war that the United States was meddling in—it was now also an American war.

The Japanese moved quickly in their attempts to snatch up territory before the American forces could recover from their losses at Pearl Harbor. Many of these territories were British possessions, so British troops rushed to defend England's lands. The British troops were no match for the ruthless Japanese soldiers, however.

"In the first six to twelve months of war with the United States and Britain, I will run wild and win victory after victory," Admiral Yamamoto had predicted before the attack on Pearl Harbor. "But then," he quietly added, "if the war continues after that, I have no expectation of success."

Yamamoto and his forces did indeed run wild in the first months. The British surrendered Hong Kong on Christmas Day, and Singapore, Burma, and Borneo fell to the Japanese within five months.

In many of these countries, the residents at first welcomed the Japanese. Japan had preceded its takeovers of these lands with a lot of propaganda.

"Asia for the Asiatics!" pamphlets proclaimed. The inhabitants of these nations, many of which had been ruled by European countries, were led to believe that the rule of Asian people should be by Asian people, not by Europeans thousands of miles away. In many ways, this made sense. And, in fact, many of these people had been mistreated and abused by their European rulers. When the Japanese first marched into these territories, people cheered.

But it didn't take very long for the citizens of these occupied territories to realize that their new rulers were no better than the European rulers had been. Often, in fact, they were much worse. The Japanese soldiers had no interest in becoming friendly with the people in the lands they took over. They had been instructed to use terror, murder, and rape as methods of intimidation. Even when given a friendly welcome, the Japanese soldiers responded with brutality. It was not unusual for the Japanese to make a big show of lining up innocent people chosen at random and massacring them.

With the battle cry of "Banzai!" the Japanese fought with a ferocity and cruelty that, some historians agree, even overshadowed the heartlessness of the Nazi soldiers. Because surrender was unacceptable to the Japanese, they would fight to the bitter end, even killing themselves before allowing their enemy to capture them. It was perhaps this disregard for their own lives in time of war that led them to have such disregard for the lives of their enemies.

The reputation of the Japanese warriors spread quickly. Soon, people in invaded lands simply surrendered immediately, often falling to the ground and begging for mercy. In the year following Pearl Harbor, the Japanese were so victorious that most of the Asian Pacific seaboard belonged to them, and it began to look as though they were planning to attack both India and Australia. Many people in Asia began to feel that, like the Nazis in Europe, the Japanese could not be stopped.

American soldiers and generals, however, felt otherwise. At the same time the Japanese attacked Pearl Harbor, they also invaded Wake Island, about 2,400 miles west of Hawaii, in the middle of the Pacific Ocean. On Wake was a small United States base with about 450 American Marines. Why would the United States care about this remote island? For the same reason the Japanese wanted it—it was positioned so that it protected the Philippines from attack. If the Japanese could take over Wake Island, they could use it as a base for their own military. Conquering the Philippines would be easy after that.

Although the Americans suffered losses in the initial surprise attack on Wake Island, they were more prepared for Japan's next strike three days later. They fired on the Japanese ships with huge coastal artillery guns and managed to sink two destroyers, blowing one of them up when the shots hit a supply of explosives on board. Although this was a small battle, it was significant because it was Japan's first defeat of the war. The Japanese retreated, but the Americans knew they would be back.

The American commander at Wake Island sent Pearl Harbor a message that was intercepted by the Japanese: "Send us more Japs!" The Japanese were furious. Was this commander making fun of them by suggesting that they were no match for the few Marines stationed on Wake? In reality, the commander had sent the message in code so that if it were intercepted, the Japanese would read only the first three words and the last word of the message. The actual message had urgently requested help, supplies, and a battleship.

Help never arrived. The commander at Pearl Harbor decided that he couldn't risk losing more ships and lives. When the Japanese attacked again twelve days later with 1,500 soldiers and a fresh fleet of ships, the Wake Island forces didn't stand a chance. Still, they fought fearlessly for a full day before finally surrendering. In the end, the terribly outnumbered Americans had killed nearly 1,000 Japanese soldiers, burned two destroyers, and shot down or damaged twenty-eight planes. Wake Island was lost, but the spirit of the American soldiers was inspirational. And the phrase "Send more Japs!" became a rallying cry for American soldiers throughout the war in the Pacific.

"Age wrinkles the body. Quitting wrinkles the soul."

Those were the words of General Douglas MacArthur, who was chosen by President Roosevelt to lead the battle against the Japanese in the Philippines. From the start, MacArthur had been placed in an unwinnable situation. Although there was a combined force of 125,000 American and Philippine soldiers, it was still no match for the Japanese. As had happened at Wake Island, MacArthur could not get the weapons and naval support he needed from Pearl Harbor. After weeks of fighting, the American troops were running out of food and ammunition. However, a steady stream of supplies—and fresh soldiers—rolled in from nearby Japan.

Yet MacArthur fought on. "Americans don't quit!" he muttered again and again, his teeth clenched around his ever-present corncob pipe. In the face of hopelessness, MacArthur refused to give up, making him a symbol of determination for the American people. Finally, however, President Roosevelt, not willing to risk losing a top general, ordered MacArthur to escape to Australia. MacArthur left reluctantly, famously announcing, "I shall return!"

What followed was one of Japan's most notorious examples of brutality. More than 75,000 soldiers (including 12,000 Americans) were cornered in a part of the Philippines known as Bataan and were taken prisoner by the Japanese. It was decided that these prisoners should march to a prison camp about seventy miles away.

The Japanese generals scoffed, saying that the distance was nothing—that their own soldiers could walk it easily.

And so began what came to be known as the Bataan Death March. For a week, the prisoners were tortured, mutilated, and starved as they moved slowly toward the camp. It was terribly hot in the Philippines in April, but the Japanese refused to give the prisoners any water. The Japanese favored torturing the prisoners by making them sit in the burning sun for hours without shade, then shooting them if they asked for a drink.

At night, the prisoners were often crammed, one on top of another, into small cargo containers. In the morning, those on the bottom were found crushed or suffocated. Along the burning roads during the day, prisoners who fell out of line or collapsed were beheaded or intentionally run over by Japanese tanks. Often the remains were left in the roads for dogs to eat. Other times, the Japanese forced prisoners to carry the mutilated bodies just to add to their misery. And following behind the prisoners were what were known as "Buzzard Squads," lines of Japanese soldiers with bayonets who would stab prisoners whose pace put them at the back of the pack.

By the time the Bataan Death March ended, nearly 15,000 soldiers had died. The grisly details of this horror ignited a fury among Americans and united them in a determination to beat the Japanese. One American admiral expressed the raw bitterness that many Americans felt when he vowed, "Before we're through with them, the Japanese language will be spoken only in hell."

It must be remembered, however, that cruelty was sometimes a two-way street. There were also reports of American soldiers shooting unarmed and wounded Japanese prisoners and turning their body parts into souvenirs, sometimes stringing teeth to make necklaces and bracelets. In the United States, anti-Japanese propaganda spread quickly with cartoons of Japanese people drawn to make them look like horrid insects and monsters. They were often portrayed as nothing more than mindless, heartless murderers. Japanese-American-owned businesses were boycotted, and "No Japs Wanted!" signs began showing up on the front doors of restaurants and stores.

Soon after the attack on Pearl Harbor, President Roosevelt ordered the internment (imprisonment) of more than 110,000 Japanese people living in the United States. Nearly all of those interned were American citizens, and none had broken any laws— they were simply considered a "threat to national security" because of their Japanese ancestry. In particular, Roosevelt was worried that the Japanese in the United States might work as spies for Japan. Some Americans, who realized that these prison camps were wrong, pointed out that over half of the internees were children. How could they possibly work as spies?

"A Jap's a Jap," the commanding general of the Western Defense Command, John DeWitt, said stubbornly, refusing, like many Americans, to see that the camps were racist and unconstitutional. "And that's all there is to it."

Though the Japanese internment camps were in no way as terrible as the concentration camps for Jews in Poland and Germany, they were still quite bad. Most of the camps were located in remote and treeless areas in the Southwest, often in the middle of a desert. They were surrounded by tall fences, barbed wire, and guards with rifles. Dozens of people were crammed together in poorly constructed metal barracks, where there was no privacy or personal space.

Nearly all the Japanese people sent to these camps lost their businesses, farms, or jobs as a result of being interned for up to four years. All of their belongings had been left behind and confiscated by the U.S. authorities, so when the prisoners were finally released, they had nothing. In the end, thousands of lives were ruined as a result of American paranoia and fear.

"I looked down the empty dirt road and at the metal houses," recalled one Japanese man, who was only 9 when his family was placed in a camp in the desert. "It was so different from our lovely home in California. And so I asked my mother what we had done wrong, and she said, 'Nothing. It's because we are Japanese.' I looked at her and said, 'But we are

Americans!' I still remember her staring off into the distance for some time. Then she looked at me and said, 'No we're not. Not until this war is over.'"

Ironically, only ten people were ever convicted of spying for Japan during World War II. All of them were white.

CHAPTER 9

Hitler couldn't wait to go to war with the United States. With all the action in the Pacific following the bombing of Pearl Harbor, some people had practically forgotten that Germany had declared war on the United States—but Hitler hadn't forgotten. While some of his military advisers hinted that it would be suicidal to go to war with America, Hitler ignored their warnings.

"They are a mongrel race," Hitler said, tossing Americans in with all the other people he didn't like. "I have no fear of *them*."

To Hitler's way of thinking, the United States had weakened itself by openly welcoming people of all nationalities, races, and religions. Its people were simply not as pure as his German master race. In his book *Mein Kampf*, Hitler praised only one aspect of the United States: the way people had taken over Native American lands and either forced Native Americans onto reservations or killed them. That he found impressive, but everything else about Americans was, in his opinion, weak and pathetic.

Furthermore, Hitler believed that, like Britain, the United States had only a strong navy to protect it. He thought that the United States' air and ground forces would be no match for Germany's. The fact that in World War I the tide had turned against Germany due to American forces didn't matter to Hitler. This was a new Germany, a Nazi Germany, free of the weak politicians and destructive Jews. And so Hitler declared war on the United States. It was, many historians believe, the biggest military mistake he would make.

As if they were revving giant engines, both the Axis and the Allies now prepared for war. However, their preparations differed greatly.

There were more than fifty countries around the world that were part of the Allied forces, but the United States, Britain, and the Soviet Union were the main players, and, as a result, they became known as "the Big Three." After Germany's surprise attack on the Soviets on June 22, 1941, Stalin had declared war on Germany, drawing him into the circle of Allies.

In many ways, it was hard to imagine Roosevelt and Stalin working together to win a war. Stalin was a Communist, a severe and often cruel leader, and a man who did not particularly enjoy sitting down and chatting about diplomacy and war strategy. He just wanted to get on with it: fight and win, regardless of the loss of life. His views were often directly opposite those of President Roosevelt, who once described

Stalin as a "devil-like tyrant leading a vile system."
As a result, Britain's Churchill often found himself
as the go-between for the two men. It was not that
Churchill was terribly fond of Stalin or approved of
Communism, but he realized, wisely, that the ability
of the Allies to work together would ultimately be
the undoing of the Axis.

And work together, they did. All three countries
went into overdrive to produce what would be
needed for the war effort, from fields of corn to
armored tanks. Millions of people worked very
hard and sacrificed a great deal. In Britain and the
United States, fuel, food, and even clothing were
rationed so that more could be sent to each nation's
soldiers. Food had already become somewhat scarce
in Britain during the months of fighting alone against
Germany, but now it would become more scarce.
When American soldiers who were living and training
in England realized how hungry many of their new
neighbors were, they often ate only half of their rations
and gave the rest away. British children became quite
fond of "the Yanks," as the U.S. soldiers were called,
who handed them packs of gum, chocolate bars, and
sandwiches.

America was terribly unprepared for such a
major war. But unlike Britain and the Soviet Union,
the United States was not being constantly attacked
and bombed by the enemy. Therefore, Americans felt
responsible for providing both themselves and their
allies with arms and supplies.

"America must become the arsenal of democracy," Roosevelt proclaimed, urging all Americans to pitch in for the war effort.

And by all Americans, Roosevelt meant *all* Americans. Because of the Great Depression, unemployment had been high for more than a decade, but now there were jobs for everyone. When millions of young men volunteered for military service, leaving their jobs behind, employers turned to those who were not usually considered for high-paying factory and technical jobs: women and African Americans. Between 1941 and 1944, the employment of both women and blacks more than tripled.

Women who had been housewives only months earlier were now working on fighter-plane assembly lines, hammering in the rivets that held the planes together. The image of the oil-covered female riveter wearing overalls and a red bandana became a national symbol during the war. Songs about "Rosie the Riveter" were written, and posters with a picture of Rosie flexing her bicep and saying "We Can Do It!" were seen from Maine to California.

The enthusiasm and patriotism on the home front worked. During the war, shipbuilding in the United States increased by 600 percent and aircraft production by 500 percent. More than 60,000 tanks were built in twenty-four months alone. By 1944, it was estimated that a new plane was built every five minutes—nearly all of them made almost entirely by female workers—and a new warship was built every day. An unbelievable level of commitment and hard work by Americans—and boosted production from the British—soon gave the Allies a serious advantage over the Axis in terms of warfare. And the Axis would never catch up.

Home front "spirit" was different in the Soviet Union. Rather than inspiring citizens to work, Stalin *forced* them to work. More than one million Soviets were sent to work camps where, among other things, they produced ammunition, gas masks, and tanks, often working eighteen hours a day—for no pay. If a worker complained, he or she could be shipped off to Siberia to die in a brutal concentration camp known as a "gulag." Added to this misery was a serious shortage of food in the Soviet Union. This was made worse by Stalin denying food to those who did not work in war-effort jobs. In time, the lack of food would be eased by help from the United States, but many Soviets would die of starvation during those difficult years.

And yet the Soviets loved their country. Their dislike of Stalin and his brutality was overshadowed by their dedication to, as many called it, "Holy Mother Russia." They would defend her to the end. And so they endured, suffered, and worked—sometimes to the death. They understood well the need to work with the Allies and combine the power of the Big Three. It was how the war would be won.

* * *

"Church, kitchen, and children," Hitler often said. "That is all women are good for."

As might be expected, Nazis believed that women were not nearly as important or useful as men. Hitler felt obligated to protect German women, to some extent, so that they could continue giving birth to the master race, but women were prohibited from filling other roles. Therefore, although the Allies filled arms factories with female workers, Hitler stubbornly refused to let a woman do a "man's job."

So as most of the German male population went off to fight, who worked in the arms factories? In Nazi Germany, nearly all of the work was done by slave laborers. Hitler ordered nearly twelve million people from surrounding countries the Nazis had conquered to work nonstop. But unlike the people who worked in Soviet factories, Hitler's slaves felt hatred, not love, for the country they were working for. Many workers intentionally broke machinery, "forgot" to tighten important bolts on planes, and made machine guns that wouldn't fire. Nearly all the slave workers were starving to death, so the threat of being killed for sabotage was not particularly effective. Although German wartime production shot up dramatically after Germany declared war on the United States, it was still not enough to keep up with the Allies' production.

Japan and Italy, the two other main Axis powers, were not very concerned about helping Germany.

Japan was basically fighting its own war. Italy was so entirely unprepared and bungling its own war efforts that it was more of a problem for Germany than a help. As Hitler grew more and more irritated with Mussolini and the Italian war effort, he finally cast Italy aside, although it remained a member of the Axis.

As for Japan's wartime production, the Japanese soon found that they had spread themselves too thin. With so much new territory to control and now a formidable new enemy to fight, the Japanese began running out of both manpower and equipment. Additionally, Japan had always depended on foreign imports to supply it with the materials needed for its planes and bombs. Now the United States Navy was blocking many of those supplies from getting into Japan.

But even if the Axis powers had had all the warfare and materials they needed, they would still have been missing a very special piece of the war puzzle that only the Allies possessed: the *willingness* to work together. Hitler's obsession with the perfection of his master race led him to disregard everyone else—even those who could help him. Furthermore, a lack of support and a level of resistance within their own countries made things even more difficult for Germany and Italy. Many Germans were disgusted by Hitler's Nazi movement, and Italians, in general, did not like Mussolini.

In conquered lands, resistance and hatred were particularly fierce. In the Pacific, those who had come under Japanese rule were often too frightened and unprepared to fight back. But this was not true in Europe. An underground group known as the French Resistance secretly laid dynamite along train tracks to blow up German military trains that carried supplies and arms through occupied France. And in Eastern Europe, roving bands of fighters known as "Partisans" hid in the forests and mountains, and sprang surprise attacks on Nazi soldiers.

The Partisans welcomed anyone who wanted to see the Nazis defeated—male, female, Jewish, gypsy—even ten-year-old boys. A ten-year-old Jewish boy named Mathei Jackel escaped a train packed with prisoners headed for a concentration camp when he jumped out at a station and ran, dodging bullets, deep into a Polish forest. He was huddled under leaves and freezing when he was discovered by a group of men in Nazi uniforms. Looking up at these soldiers, Mathei thought he would be shot immediately. Instead, one of the men helped Mathei to his feet and gave him food and a warm blanket.

"We are Partisans," the man explained. "We wear these uniforms as a disguise."

Mathei, stunned with relief, just nodded.

"The Germans reserve a special hatred for us Partisans," the man continued in a low voice. "If we are captured, we face a fate worse than death.

We are tortured, often for days, until we give up our secrets."

The man looked carefully at Mathei. Mathei was just a child, but he had been brave enough to jump off a train and run through bullets to save his own life and escape the Nazis.

"Would you like to be one of us?" the man finally asked. Mathei, who was still speechless, just nodded again.

For the next two years, Mathei traveled through Poland and into the Soviet Union with the Partisans. Before he was even eleven years old, he had lit fuses that led to dynamite beneath German tanks. He had carried a revolver and a machine gun and used them often. If Mathei ever showed fear, he was told to "grow up."

"I'm just a kid, and I don't deserve any of this," Mathei often thought as he fought with the Partisans. Even so, the horrific actions of the Nazis spurred him on. Word had spread that more and more people were dying in the concentration camps. Children and women were the first to die. And once, while sneaking through fields in an occupied section of western Soviet Union, the Partisans came upon a pile of corpses of children. Every one of them was a ghostly white; they had been drained of blood.

"These children were murdered for blood transfusions for wounded German soldiers," one of the Partisans explained grimly. "Do you see why we must continue our fight?"

Mathei would survive the war and his time as a Partisan, but like so many children caught up in this terrible time, he would lose something very precious—namely, his childhood.

Lack of Axis cooperation, dwindling supplies, increasing resistance in occupied countries—all of these problems should have been warnings to Hitler. As a man who was often described as a brilliant, if evil, dictator, how could he have missed these signs? Specifically, Hitler refused to ever acknowledge that the Germans could be beaten. He had had several years of tremendous military success, and now it was merely time to finish the job. But the job had become overwhelming.

German armies were now fighting for territories in eastern Europe, North Africa, and the Middle East. In addition, German U-boats and battleships patrolled the Atlantic Ocean in search of American and British warships. The Battle of the Atlantic was particularly frightening for the Allies at first. Submarines were a relatively new type of war vessel. They had been used in World War I, but they had been perfected for World War II. Now they were able to sneak up on the Allies' ships late at night and destroy them with torpedoes.

However, the Allies quickly developed a new and improved form of sonar that enabled them to better detect the oncoming U-boats. It was so effective that before long, two out of three German submarines were sunk before they could even get the British and American vessels in their sights. German sailors soon became afraid to serve on U-boats.

"What once were great war ships," one German sailor said of their submarines, "are now just iron coffins."

Still, Hitler would not back down, change direction, or consider his errors. In his mind, everything was going according to his great plan. There was, however, one problem that continued to nag at Hitler: what to do about the Jews. Every day, thousands of Jews were being transported to concentration camps where, according to plan, they would be worked, beaten, or starved to death. But the plan seemed to be moving too slowly for Hitler's tastes. So, early in 1942, Hitler came up with what he called "the Final Solution to the Jewish Question."

Time would no longer be wasted waiting around for the Jews to die. Now Hitler ordered the immediate mass murder of all Jews. Concentration camps became death factories. After all, Hitler explained, the Jews had caused this Second World War. They deserved such a fate. Hitler's propaganda minister, Joseph Goebbels, chillingly explained the situation:

"Regarding the Jewish Question, the Führer is determined to clear the table. He warned the Jews that if they were to cause another world war, it would lead to their own destruction. Those were not empty words. Now the world war has come. The destruction of the Jews must be its necessary consequence. We cannot be sentimental about it. It is not for us to feel sympathy for the Jews."

The Holocaust had begun.

CHAPTER 10

Auschwitz. Chelmno. Belzec. Majdanek. Sobibor. Treblinka.

These were the names of the six death camps the Nazis set up in remote parts of Poland. Inside the barbed-wire and electric fences staggered thousands of human skeletons dressed in ragged striped uniforms. Beyond them, dark billowing smoke that smelled of death rose nearly twenty-four hours a day. White ash, like dirty snow, covered the ground. Screams of women rang out, children cried, and desperate men threw themselves against the deadly electric fences every day in an attempt to end the horror sooner.

The Nazis hid these camps well. They didn't want German citizens to see them for fear of "upsetting" their refined tastes. And they knew the Allies would have been horrified to learn what was going on and would have interrupted Hitler's Final Solution. There were millions of Jews to kill—the process must run smoothly, quietly, and quickly.

The first step was getting the Jews to the death camps. More Jews lived in Poland than in any other country, so there it was a simple matter of gathering them up and shipping them off. The Nazis decided that this could be done with the most secrecy and efficiency if the Jews were packed into windowless cattle cars and sent by railway. So railroad tracks were laid directly into the six camps, where the unloading of the cars could be hidden behind the tall walls. Once the tracks were in place, "deportation," as it was called, began.

"My brother died in my arms," recalled a Jewish woman known only as Helen. "There was not enough oxygen for all those people in the cars. The Nazis kept us in those cattle cars for days. . . . They hoped we would die there before we got to the camps."

Crammed together in complete darkness with no idea where they were headed, the deported Jews stood silently at first. Some cried without making a sound. Many of them prayed. All of them were terrified. There was no room to move at all. Occasionally, the trains would stop briefly, and those inside the cars could hear the guards shouting. Footsteps would approach, and the doors would slide open for just a minute, allowing barely a breath of fresh air to enter. Then more Jews would be packed in, and the train would take off again.

No food or water was given to the deportees, and often the heat of the day literally roasted people alive inside the cattle cars. Human waste covered the floors, along with the bodies of the dead. A woman named Gertrude Levi, who was deported from Hungary, recalled that the Nazi guards often stood laughing at the packed cars. Occasionally, they would hand out terribly dry biscuits, knowing that the prisoners were starving but that their throats were too dry to swallow anything.

"This made people go into hysterics," Gertrude remembered. "We had the dead, the mad, the hysterical, and the screaming among us, and we could not do a thing about it."

When the trains finally creaked to a stop at their destinations, a new kind of hell awaited those on board.

"Get in line! Get in Line!" Nazi guards screamed at the confused and frightened prisoners. The dead were pulled off the train and thrown on a truck that would take them to be buried, without ceremony, in a big pit. Those who had survived the trip were directed to form a long line. One by one, they were roughly checked the way a veterinarian might check a farm animal. After their teeth were poked, their muscles prodded, and their hair pulled, they were sent to a group either on the left or on the right.

This was known as "selection." Many prisoners, particularly old people, pregnant women, and children, were not checked at all. They were just immediately directed toward the group on the left.

"I remember thinking that the group to the left was the group to get placed in," recalled a young man named David Baker. "Those were the weak, the fragile women, the children, the old. I think many of us thought that they were going to be treated better, maybe not sent to the hard labor jobs the rest of us expected."

David was wrong. He watched the group disappear behind a building, and then he never saw any of those people again. As for David, he and his group, mostly young men and a few women, were sent to work. Although Hitler wanted all Jews killed, he still needed slave labor to produce supplies for the war effort. Also, he used Jews for jobs around the death camps that he felt were too exhausting and grisly for the Nazi soldiers.

One young Polish Jewish woman named Kitty Hart discovered what David had not seen. She was assigned night work in the kitchen at Auschwitz, cooking for the soldiers. During the day, she was ordered to stay in the filthy and poorly constructed bunker (or prison building) where she and dozens of other women slept on lice-infested wooden slats. Each woman's only possessions were one dirty striped uniform, to be worn twenty-four hours a day, and a metal bowl. The bowl was used both as a soup bowl at mealtime, and, when prisoners were not allowed to leave the bunkers, as a toilet. Because it was their only personal belonging, many prisoners scratched their names on these bowls and slept with them under their heads so that no one could steal them. Rats and mice often ran over the women, nibbling at their feet and at raw sores on their bodies.

This was certainly a monstrous existence, but then Kitty saw something one day, as she peered out the tiny window in the bunker, that made her wonder if she was one of the lucky ones. Kitty recalled that she had a direct view of the new prisoners coming into Auschwitz.

"I saw that the women and children had been separated, as usual, from most of the men. They were led to a small field where the children would pick flowers, and the women would share whatever small bits of food they still had. It was as if they thought they were on some kind of picnic."

It all seemed innocent enough, but what Kitty observed next made her physically sick. Part of the group was suddenly led into a low brick building, and a heavy door was slammed and bolted shut. Kitty could hear some muffled shouting.

"Then I could see a person walking up a ladder wearing a gas mask," Kitty recalled. "He would empty a tin into an opening at the top of the building, and then he would run down the ladder very quickly."

The next moment, Kitty could hear screams. Then after several minutes had passed, there was complete silence.

Sometime later, a dark, putrid smoke came from the tall chimney at the opposite end of the same low building. Kitty suddenly realized that the building was both a gas chamber and a crematorium for burning the corpses. Soon workers were seen pushing cartloads of ash from the building and dumping the ash into the nearby pond. Once all these steps had been completed, two guards casually walked back to the small field and ordered another hundred or so people to follow them.

"What I couldn't understand," Kitty said, "was that the people sitting in the field were totally calm. They had no idea that the people who had gone in front of them were already dead. They simply had no idea."

The use of a type of poisonous gas known as "Zyklon B" became the Nazis' preferred method of murder. It was quick, did not require the use of ammunition, and, perhaps of greatest importance to the Nazis, enabled them to kill thousands of people every day. Some gas chambers were large enough to hold more than 2,000 victims per gassing. Furthermore, the awful work of hauling the bodies to the long rows of ovens where they were cremated, and then dumping the ash, could be done by Jewish prisoners. Even the dangerous job of dropping the canister of poisonous gas into the chamber was performed by a prisoner. It appealed to Hitler's dark humor to think that, technically, Jews were killing Jews.

Although rumors had spread among Jewish people about mass murder through the use of gas, many found it hard to imagine or believe that anyone, even the Nazis, could be that evil. If prisoners were nervous as they were being led to the gas chambers, the guards would often reassure them that they were simply being taken to showers. And, as bizarre as it seems, upbeat music was often played over loudspeakers to give a false sense of optimism. Guards would instruct the prisoners to undress for their "showers," piling clothing in one stack and shoes in another. It was not until the prisoners found themselves packed into a dark room with no showers in sight, and heard the heavy door slam, that they realized the truth.

"The stacks of shoes behind the gas chambers were sometimes taller than the building itself," remembered one prisoner, whose job it had been to sort shoes. "I'd look at the worn soles of the shoes sometimes and think, 'So many miles walked in these shoes. No more.' But really the worst were the tiny children's shoes. So few miles on those shoes."

Prisoners who were not "selected" for immediate death by gassing faced a slower kind of death. Some, mostly young men, remained in the killing camps, doing all the work connected to the mass murders. At times when the gas chambers were too crowded, Nazi guards would force these prisoners to dig deep pits. Then women and children would be lined along the pits and shot so that they would fall backward into the mass grave. Male prisoners who had been forced to dig these graves were also forced to watch the shootings. Many of these women and children were only wounded, not killed, but it had become a Nazi policy to "waste no more than two bullets per prisoner."

"And so then we had to pile the dirt back on top of the bodies," a prisoner remembered with disgust. "Some were not dead, and these were crying out, children screaming! You could see them moving beneath the dirt. No matter. We had to bury them alive or face the bullets ourselves."

Other prisoners were sent to work camps, where they were forced to do backbreaking and often dangerous work for eighteen hours a day with practically no food. At the entrance to many of these camps hung large signs that read "Arbeit Macht Frei" (German for "Work will free you"). Of course, the cruel irony—which the Nazis realized all too plainly—was that the work would kill the prisoners. Before the Final Solution, some work camps had made attempts to keep prisoners alive so that as much slave labor as possible could be drawn from them before they died. Now the sooner they died, the better.

Nearly everything done at the work camps was intended to make the lives of the prisoners more miserable. Often awakened at 2:30 in the morning, prisoners were made to stand in long rows in the barren prison yard for roll call. Sometimes these roll calls took four hours or more. In pouring rain or bitter winter storms, prisoners were made to stand absolutely still in their threadbare uniforms and bare feet. If a prisoner collapsed, he or she would be beaten or shot. Often, a guard would intentionally lose his place in the roll so that the process would have to start all over again. At day's end, when the prisoners were exhausted from work, roll call was demanded once more. If even one person was absent, roll call could go on all night.

Food was another misery. A typical meal consisted of a crust of moldy bread, a small piece of rotting salami, and warm brownish water that the guards laughingly called "Jew coffee." Camp cooks were instructed to keep the food both unhealthy and scarce. Prisoners were so desperate for any kind of nourishment that they would eat the grass and weeds growing in the prison yard.

"Eaten down to the dirt," a prisoner at Belzec remembered. "The grass never grew in the camp. I never remember seeing any green at Belzec. In fact, I don't remember ever seeing the sun. The sun must have shined, but I don't remember one day that didn't seem dark."

Added to this was the cruelty of the guards who enjoyed playing their "games," as they called them, with prisoners. They taunted them by leaving food where it could be reached, then whipping prisoners who reached for it. During roll call, a guard would knock a man's hat off his head, putting the man in a terrible dilemma. Prisoners could be shot for not wearing a hat—and shot for stepping out of line during roll call. Guards would yell for the man to put on his hat and then laugh at his confusion and fear. Stand still or pick up the hat—either way, the prisoner would be shot.

And nearly every day, a prisoner or two was pulled aside for "medical experiments." These were horrific and very painful procedures carried out by the German camp physicians. One doctor in particular, Dr. Mengele, was nicknamed "the Angel of Death" because of his deadly experiments. Mengele, who worked at Auschwitz, favored using children for his research. During his years at Auschwitz, he injected chemicals directly into children's eyes to see if they would change color. He shot gasoline into veins just to see what the reaction would be. And once he sewed two children together in an attempt to "create" conjoined twins. Nearly all of his subjects died.

"Mengele ran a butcher shop," said an Auschwitz prisoner who had witnessed some of Mengele's experiments. "He was a doctor who became insane because of the power he was given. . . . Nobody ever questioned him. He did as he pleased without regard to the fact that his experiments were no more than deadly torture."

During these years of the Final Solution, millions of Jews were slaughtered. As the Allies pushed closer to Poland, the Nazis began speeding up the killing process, fearing that their murder factories would be discovered before every Jew had been killed. Mountains of gassed corpses waiting to be burned were piled throughout the death camps. In some camps, impatient commanders simply ordered thousands of prisoners to be thrown alive onto giant bonfires.

In time, this was the period that would become known as "the Holocaust," from a Greek word meaning "sacrifice by fire."

Everything imaginable was done to make the prisoners of the Holocaust feel lifeless and worthless. Numbers were tattooed on their forearms or wrists to strip them of their identity. They were starved, humiliated, raped, beaten, and enslaved. The Nazis wanted the Jews, gypsies, Poles, Soviets, homosexuals, and all others they deemed "unfit for life" to lose all hope. They wanted to destroy the very last shreds of desire to survive.

And yet there were those who would *never* give up.

"Every morning at 3:30," wrote a former Auschwitz prisoner, "I had a ten-minute talk with God—not because I was afraid. I demanded to know what He had done to His people, why He was doing this. And then I demanded to be liberated, because I wanted to live."

CHAPTER 11

Where to begin? That was the big question President Roosevelt was tackling in the summer of 1942. There was a lot of war to choose from. Germany was pushing farther into the Soviet Union; the British were still living under the threat of Nazi invasion; North Africa was seeing more and more attacks from Germany and Italy; Japan had attacked the United States; and people in China and the South Pacific who suffered under the Japanese were looking to the Allies for help.

Most Americans were in agreement: We must go after Japan first. The Japanese military had sprung a ruthless surprise attack on sleeping troops, killing thousands. They had destroyed a good chunk of our Pacific fleet. It was now a matter of restoring our pride and seeking revenge. In addition, if we didn't fight back quickly, Japan would be given the chance to strengthen its defenses by taking over more of China and using more of China's resources and labor.

However, the British were not in agreement with the Americans. Sure, Hitler was taking a break from bombing England, but the Nazis had nearly destroyed London before taking a breather. And now, as they chipped away at the Soviet Union, there was a growing sense of dread in England. What if Hitler *did* manage to conquer the Soviets? Certainly, his next stop would be a return to England to finish off Europe altogether. If the Americans wasted precious time restoring their injured pride in the Pacific, Europe could be lost to the Nazis.

Then Winston Churchill brought up another problem: Unless the Americans helped the British fight German forces in North Africa (mostly in the African countries of Libya and Egypt), there was a chance that the Germans would take over the all-important Suez Canal. This small canal was Britain's gateway to India and the rest of Asia, and many resources that the British depended on traveled through this canal. German control of the Suez could cripple Great Britain, since supplies would have to travel around the southern tip of Africa, a trip that was thousands of miles longer. Controlling the Suez Canal would give Germany a significant advantage.

Furthermore, Churchill believed that because of its position directly south of Italy and central Europe, North Africa would be the perfect spot for launching the Allies' attack against the Axis.

"North Africa is the soft underbelly of the Axis," Churchill often repeated, meaning that, in his opinion, it was the Axis's weakest point.

The Germans would expect an Allied attack to be launched from England, not Africa. Therefore, Churchill tried to persuade Roosevelt to send American troops to first defeat the Nazis and Italians in North Africa and then use the African coast as the Allies' attack base.

Complicating things even more for Roosevelt was the situation in the Soviet Union. Now that the weather was beginning to warm, the Germans were attacking in full force, slaughtering thousands of Soviets and taking over more and more of the western edge of the Soviet Union. Stalin was not that upset over the loss of Soviet lives—life, to Stalin, was expendable. But he was seriously upset over the thought of losing his country. Making matters worse, Stalin was a bit paranoid. He didn't trust capitalists, and he believed that Roosevelt and Churchill were secretly plotting against both the Soviets and the Germans, hoping that both sides would wear themselves out fighting each other. Then, Stalin thought bitterly, the capitalists would take over.

With people pulling him in so many different directions, Roosevelt finally had enough. He was commander in chief, and he would command. "Focus on Germany first, and then defeat Japan" was his decision. It was a decision that angered many Americans and stunned his military advisers. Not immediately go after the country that attacked *us*? Unthinkable! But Roosevelt had his reasons.

Roosevelt sensed that in many ways Hitler and the Nazis were a much more dangerous threat, both to Americans and to the world, than were the Japanese. Also, Joseph Stalin was a rather unstable and unpredictable leader. Roosevelt and Churchill worried that Stalin would switch sides and strike a deal with Hitler if American forces didn't show their support and start fighting the Germans pretty quickly. And the military powerhouse combination of Germany and the Soviet Union would be terrifying indeed. Furthermore, Churchill felt it was very important for the Allies to be united at the beginning, working together against Hitler. Even though Churchill was no fan of Communism and was directly opposed to many of Stalin's beliefs and practices, he believed, correctly, that Adolf Hitler was far more dangerous than Stalin.

So the decision was made, and a plan was put in place. As Churchill had wished, American troops would begin the war against the Germans in North Africa, hoping to get to the Nazis through that vulnerable "soft underbelly."

Fighting battles in the flat, wide-open deserts of North Africa was a different kind of experience for both the Allies and the Axis. For the German troops and their leader, General Erwin Rommel, it was at first as close as war could get to being "fun." Rommel had been the extremely successful general in charge when Germany had humiliated France into surrendering in only a matter of weeks. Now Rommel roared across the desert in a huge tank, so confident of the German troops' superiority over the British that he actually directed his troops from the frontlines. To Rommel, the desert was like the ocean. No naval victory was ever won from the shoreline, so Rommel, like a navy admiral, stood at the front, risking his own life.

Rommel was so cunning and successful at desert warfare that his troops nicknamed him "the Desert Fox." Not only was Rommel brave and cunning; he was also a different kind of German war leader. He fought strictly for the honor of his homeland, never because of hatred for other people. In addition, Rommel always discouraged cruel treatment of the enemy by his own troops. Although Hitler commanded him to do so, Rommel refused to execute prisoners simply because they were Jewish. And when a British major was killed during a failed raid to capture Rommel behind German lines, Rommel personally ordered the major to be buried with full military honors.

"It is a war without hate," Rommel said of the war in North Africa.

Still, it was not a war without death, terror, and destruction. For some time, the Desert Fox and the Germans held the upper hand. Then the war seemed to move in favor of the British and their moody, short-tempered general, Bernard Montgomery. Rommel became more and more frustrated. How could a war out in the middle of nowhere, with no buildings, no civilians, and no complications, be taking so long to win? Originally, Rommel had predicted that this unusual war in a desert would be over, as the war in France had been, in a few weeks.

Finally, Rommel and his troops found themselves so threatened that they surrounded themselves with miles of booby traps and hidden explosives. Known as "the Devil's Garden," this minefield was Rommel's last gasp in the North African war. British troops picked their way across the Devil's Garden and launched a thousand-gun bombardment that was so loud and frightening that it actually gave one of the German commanders a fatal heart attack.

The final blow came when American troops, commanded by Dwight D. Eisenhower, finally landed in Morocco and Algeria in November 1942. Now the German troops were trapped between the British and the Americans. Rommel sent word to Hitler that the situation was hopeless, and he requested permission for German troops to retreat.

"Never!" Hitler wrote back in a fury. "Victory or death."

Rommel continued fighting for a while, but sacrificing the lives of his men just to please Hitler's sense of pride was not his style. Again he went against the Führer's orders and retreated. After retreating farther and farther (1,750 miles!), Rommel finally surrendered. It was the first time the Germans had lost. The loss in North Africa was not critical to the Germans—they had, after all, been drawn into this battle to help the floundering Italian forces. Conquering Africa was of no particular interest to Hitler. Still, it was a small turning point.

"This is not the end," Winston Churchill commented on November 10, 1942, after the historic surrender in North Africa. "It is not even the beginning of the end. But it is, perhaps, the end of the beginning."

The Allies looked north from the coast of Africa. Only 90 miles away was Sicily, the large island near the "toe" of the boot-shaped peninsula of Italy. If the Allies could take over this Italian island, they would be in an excellent position to attack mainland Italy and then move farther north to Germany.

Entering an Axis country, the Americans and British knew they would be badly outnumbered. The 180,000 Allied troops immediately faced 230,000 Italian troops—and 40,000 German troops were on the way to help the Italians. After about ten days of fighting, something unexpected happened: The Italians surrendered. Essentially, the Italian soldiers were tired of fighting for a dictator they didn't even like. Once a powerful and feared leader, Mussolini now was mostly an irritation to Italians, who wanted him kicked out of office. The Allies were victorious in Sicily, easily defeating the remaining German troops. Quickly, the Allies moved on to the Italian peninsula.

Although Mussolini had pleaded with Hitler to send more German troops, Hitler, much like the Italian people, had had enough of Benito Mussolini.

"Germany can no longer be expected to provide assistance," Hitler replied abruptly. "All our troops are committed to the Soviet front."

So much for the Axis countries standing by one another.

When Mussolini returned to Rome, he found that he had already been replaced. The new premier, Marshal Pietro Badoglio, ordered Mussolini to a remote mountain location, where he was isolated with no chance of trying to strike up a new deal with Hitler. And just as quickly, Badoglio began making secret peace agreements with England and the United States. Now Italy, which bordered land that Germany had already overtaken, was on the side of the Allies.

In Berlin, Hitler paced nervously, cursing his generals and fretting over his endless maps. Things were beginning to unravel right at the time Hitler had thought he was preparing to sew up all of Europe. Now, he thought, the Nazis must not back down in any way in the Soviet Union. If they captured this tremendous country and its millions of inhabitants, they could virtually be guaranteed victory over the Allies. But if they lost . . . Hitler would not allow himself to even consider that dreadful option.

By late 1942, Hitler began closing himself off in his own little world of self-importance and dreams. He no longer trusted the advice of his generals, and he felt that he was the only person who understood what it would take for the Germans to be victorious. Few would stand up to Hitler, and none dared point out to him that he was wrong. It was then that Hitler began making some serious mistakes.

As German troops pushed deeper into the Soviet Union, they enjoyed moderate success at first, easily defeating the ragged Soviet troops as their panzer tanks roared across a flat open area known as the Russian steppe. The plan was to keep moving quickly and then attack Moscow, the Soviet capital, with a sudden fury. Once Moscow and the country's government fell, so would the Soviet Union.

Then, without so much as a hint of warning, Hitler changed the plan.

"Stalingrad!" Hitler barked to his generals, slapping a map with a long stick. "Stalingrad and the Caucasus oil fields. If we capture this area, oil flow will be cut off to all of the Soviet Union. Without fuel, they will no longer be able to fight us."

In many ways, this was a bold idea. Stalingrad, an important industrial city along the Volga River, produced nearly all of the country's military supplies. The nearby oil fields were the lifeblood of the country. However, Hitler's plan was flawed. It split the German army in two, weakening it. And because Stalingrad was so much farther away than Moscow, German troops began running out of food and supplies just as another brutal Soviet winter was approaching.

Still, the German General Friedrich von Paulus predicted that Stalingrad would fall in little more than a day. He was wrong. Once again, the Soviet civilians fought as bravely as the soldiers. Stalin had sent strict instructions to his general, Vasily Chuikov, to order all the residents of Stalingrad to remain in the city and fight.

"We shall hold the city or we shall die there!" was Chuikov's obedient reply. And those living in Stalingrad, faithful to their country to the end, chanted, "There is no land beyond the Volga!" meaning that Stalingrad, on the Volga River, was the end of the line; the Germans would go no farther.

The Battle of Stalingrad was terrible and gruesome. Nearly 600 German bomber planes swarmed the city in the first two days, dropping endless bombs and reducing Stalingrad to piles of bricks and burned-out buildings. So many fires burned that the night sky remained a glowing blood-red for nearly a week. About 40,000 Soviets were killed in this first phase of the attack.

The next phase involved block-by-block fighting amid the rubble. Many of the people living in Stalingrad fought with little more than knives, rocks, and bare fists. These were no match for tanks, machine guns, and bombs.

Still, as before, the Soviets would not retreat or surrender. The German soldiers may have been better armed, but the ruins of the once-great city provided excellent spots for Soviet snipers to pick off approaching troops. And as the German troops became more and more exhausted, the Soviets brought in wave after wave of soldiers from the east. The loss of Soviet life was unthinkably high, yet the battle raged on.

Then the Soviets began to lay the trap. Chuikov ordered a steady stream of soldiers and supplies, stockpiling both for weeks. Many of these supplies and arms came from Britain and the United States and were secretly floated down the Volga River to hidden docks near Stalingrad. In time, Chuikov had more than one million troops, 15,000 pieces of artillery, 1,000 aircraft, and 1,400 tanks. He positioned all this war power to encircle an entire German army. At this point in the battle, the Germans were running low on well-trained soldiers. While they received reinforcements from Romania, Italy, Hungary, and Croatia, those soldiers were poorly equipped and poorly trained. In addition, many of them did not even want to fight for Germany—and certainly did not want to die for a country many of them despised. It was the moment of weakness the Soviets had been waiting for.

General Paulus had become a nervous wreck even before his troops were caught in what would become known as "the Bear Trap." He had developed an uncontrollable tic in one eye, and he was often seen pacing and mumbling and pulling frantically at his hair. Now the first subzero nights were freezing his troops, and heavy snowfall covered the camps. When Paulus received the news that his 250,000 soldiers were hopelessly surrounded by more than a million Soviets, he immediately sat down and wrote to Hitler: "Army heading for disaster. It is essential to withdraw all our divisions."

In Berlin, Hitler raged and slammed his fist on the table.

"I will not abandon the Volga!" he screamed. Then he sent a brief and direct response to General Paulus: "You will remain in your position and hold it at all cost."

CHAPTER 12

Hitler was more furious than anyone had ever seen him. There was no way he could allow the Soviets to push the German troops back at this point. Hitler raved at his military advisers (even though it had been *his* decision to attack Stalingrad) and blamed them for the situation the troops were in. Hermann Goering, the Nazi Luftwaffe commander, looked carefully at the map of the area where General Paulus and his 250,000 troops were trapped.

"We could fly in all the supplies and ammunition Paulus needs," Goering said confidently. "There will be no need for any surrender."

Hitler thought this was a fabulous idea. In fact, it was a ridiculous idea. In terms of simple math alone, it was easy to see that it was not possible. Every day, the troops would require 150 tons of food, 250 tons of ammunition, and 120 tons of fuel. That would take 235 planes a day, every day. But neither Hitler nor Goering bothered to look at any of those annoying details, and they immediately ordered planes to Stalingrad. The battle would go on.

It was a disaster. From November to January, 800 German planes were shot down in their attempts to deliver supplies. The wicked Siberian winter kept many planes from landing, and those that did make it never brought more than about one-tenth of what was needed. Week by week, Paulus's troops became sicker and hungrier. Every night, men froze to death. Again, Paulus asked Hitler for permission to retreat, and again Hitler said no. As the situation grew desperate, Hitler began reminding Paulus that he was expected to commit suicide before giving in to surrender.

When the German troops reached the breaking point, Hitler ordered waves of panzer tanks to attempt to break through the Soviet lines to bring aid to the soldiers. The tanks got within 30 miles of Paulus and his army before they were turned back by an overwhelming Soviet counterattack. Now the trapped Germans were on their own. There would be no more help—and no word from Hitler allowing them to retreat. Paulus refused to go against the Führer's orders, so he and his men remained as the Bear Trap tightened and tightened. Finally, on February 2, 1943, Paulus was physically forced to surrender. Of the more than 250,000 soldiers he had started with, most were already dead or dying, and now the remaining 90,000 had been captured. Paulus did not have a choice—he could no longer fight back.

Hitler, however, was relentless. Instead of

praising his general for fighting to the end, he referred to him as a coward for giving in to surrender rather than taking his own life. But Paulus would eventually have the last word. Taken as a prisoner by the Soviets, Paulus would ultimately turn against Germany and the Nazis, encouraging other German troops to do the same. At first, many in Germany thought of Paulus as a traitor, but in time many came to consider him a hero.

By the end of the Battle of Stalingrad, there were more than 750,000 casualties on each side, "casualties" including killed, injured, and missing soldiers. The Soviets actually lost more soldiers than the Germans did. Stalingrad was in ruins, and of the 250,000 soldiers led by Paulus, barely 5,000 returned to Germany. Nearly half died on a forced march to a prison in the wasteland of Siberia. It had been a terribly brutal six months of war—but against all odds the Soviets had won, and this was monumental. It was the first time the Germans had suffered a serious defeat. If the Allies' victory in North Africa had been "the end of the beginning" of World War II in Europe, the victory in Stalingrad was the beginning of the end.

Roosevelt's decision may have been to win the war in Europe first and then focus on the war in the Pacific, but this didn't mean that the Allies just sat back and ignored the Japanese—far from it. After suffering some early defeats in the Pacific, the

United States Navy regrouped and made a new plan. Perhaps it would be better, at first, simply to shake up the Japanese and catch them off-guard. After all, the Japanese military believed that no one, not even the United States, could get by it or intimidate it.

So in 1942, the undamaged aircraft carriers in Pearl Harbor took off toward scattered Japanese bases throughout the Pacific. Under the direction of Admiral Charles Nimitz, pilots took off from the decks of the ships, often many miles from the small Japanese island bases. Suddenly, seemingly out of nowhere and with no warning, U.S. bombers would swoop down over the Japanese bases, dropping bombs and then disappearing back out to sea. Since these were quick attacks by just a few planes, not much physical damage was done. But the mental damage to the Japanese was significant. Suddenly the Japanese forces were on edge and on the defensive.

After several months of these raids, the Americans grew restless. How much greater stress would it cause the Japanese if U.S. bombers could actually sneak into Japan? If bombers could some-how cross into Japan undetected, an attack on Tokyo—the country's capital and the home of Emperor Hirohito—would be a major morale boost-er for the Allies. And so a daring plan was launched.

Lieutenant Colonel James Doolittle had always had the reputation as something of a daredevil. He seemed like the perfect man to oversee what would become known as "the Doolittle Raid." Sixteen modified B-25 bombers were transported on an aircraft carrier to about 700 miles from the Japanese coast. These were big, lumbering planes that raised the blood pressure of even the most experienced pilot when he had to take off from the deck of a ship. Sixteen pilots, including Doolittle, prayed that their planes would gain enough speed on the ship's tiny runway to head up into the sky instead of down into the Pacific. And that was the easy part of the plan.

When Doolittle and his crew took off on that gray April morning in 1942, they knew they would not be returning to the carrier ship. The bombers could carry only enough fuel to get them a little past Japan—maybe. The plan called for the pilots to land on friendly airfields in China, but making it to China was a big gamble.

At first, the Doolittle Raid went as planned. Targets were hit, and the Japanese were taken totally by surprise. The targets in Japan were military and supply bases, not civilian areas, and the bombs were incendiary bombs, meaning that they were intended to start fires, not cause huge explosions. This first attack on Japan was mainly intended to frighten, not destroy.

Then night fell. The planes did not have enough fuel to reach the Chinese airfields. One by one, the pilots and their crews either parachuted out of their dying planes or attempted crash landings.

Two men drowned off the coast of China, and eight were captured by the Japanese and sent to prisons, where they were tortured and starved. Three of the captured men were killed, one of them died, and the other four were released after the war ended.

The Japanese bragged about capturing the pilots and scoffed at the Doolittle Raid, calling it "the Do-Nothing Raid." However, the raid had achieved exactly what it had intended: It had scared the Japanese very badly, whether or not they would admit it.

"The Japanese had been told they were invulnerable," Doolittle explained. "An attack on the Japanese homeland would cause confusion in the minds of the Japanese people and sow doubt about the reliability of their leaders. There was a second, equally important, psychological reason for this attack. . . . Americans badly needed a morale boost."

The Doolittle Raid had shown the Japanese that Americans were ready to fight, and it had shown Americans that their troops had what it would take to fight in the Pacific.

Perhaps most troubled of all after the Doolittle Raid was Japan's Admiral Yamamoto. The United States Navy had pulled off a sneak attack, just as the Japanese navy had done at Pearl Harbor. It was time, Yamamoto decided, to come up with a new kind of plan. Yamamoto was certain that if he could draw the United States' remaining fleet at Pearl Harbor into battle, the Japanese navy could destroy it. He knew that new warships and aircraft carriers were being built in the United States even as he sat pondering this plan. He knew that he must act quickly if he wanted to wipe out the American presence in the Pacific.

Midway Island was a small American-owned island about 1,200 miles northwest of the Hawaiian Islands. It had never particularly interested Yamamoto, but now he saw that it could be quite valuable. Yamamoto knew that if the Japanese attacked Midway, the remaining U.S. fleet from Pearl Harbor would rush to defend it. Then Yamamoto's giant armada, waiting and strategically placed, would sink every vessel. The Japanese fleet consisted of more than 200 warships. As far as Yamamoto knew, the remaining fleet at Pearl Harbor was fewer than fifty warships. How could Japan lose?

His confidence would have been knocked down a few pegs if Yamamoto had known that well before the Japanese fleet even began heading toward Midway, Admiral Charles Nimitz in Pearl Harbor was well aware of the "secret" plan. The code used in Japanese war messages had been cracked by United States intelligence some time earlier, and now Nimitz and his navy were a step ahead of the Japanese.

Nimitz and Rear Admiral Raymond Spruance quickly put together a fleet of forty-eight vessels and left for Midway. Some of the vessels were barely limping along, still under repair from other battles. Spruance knew that his navy would be terribly outnumbered and overpowered by the Japanese warships, but the Americans had a significant advantage: They would ruin Yamamoto's surprise by surprising him first! So as the impressive Japanese armada crept stealthily toward Midway, the Americans were already waiting about 200 miles from the island.

At first things did not go well for the Americans. After an initial mild strike on Midway to lure the American fleet from Pearl Harbor, a Japanese scout plane reported to a stunned Yamamoto that the Americans were already within striking range. Admiral Spruance did not want to give Yamamoto any time to plan a second attack, so he immediately sent 155 bomber planes in the direction of the Japanese armada—and straight into tragedy. A screen of Japanese Zeroes (often called the best fighter airplanes of World War II) was already in place, acting as a shield for the armada. Nearly all the American planes were shot down, sending them crashing into the Pacific.

Yamamoto was thrilled. He knew the Americans had only two aircraft carriers, since the Japanese had badly damaged the two other Pacific carriers in the earlier Battle of the Coral Sea. According to Yamamoto's calculations, this meant that the Americans could not possibly have enough planes to fight back. As a result, Yamamoto and his pilots took a break in the fighting, waiting for all the planes to return to the Japanese carriers before making the next attack plan.

Yamamoto's calculations had been wrong. One of the damaged American ships was the carrier *Yorktown*. It had been beaten up pretty badly in the Battle of the Coral Sea, but crews had worked nonstop to prepare it for the Battle of Midway. The *Yorktown* carried far more planes than Yamamoto had anticipated, and now Yamamoto's delay in the fighting was all Spruance needed to give his American sailors the advantage. Fifty U.S. dive bombers climbed above the cover of the clouds. In a screaming flash, all fifty bombers descended and tore past a disorganized screen of Zeroes just getting into position. Bomb after bomb exploded on the Japanese armada. One after another, the Japanese carriers were hit until all four had sunk to the bottom of the ocean. And along with the carriers went thousands of men and hundreds of aircraft. By nightfall, the Americans had claimed victory.

Like the Allies' victory in Stalingrad, this was a turning point. It was not just a lost battle for the Japanese; the Battle of Midway had taken many of Japan's best pilots, and it had seriously crippled the Japanese navy. Perhaps, as Yamamoto had predicted, the Japanese military had "run wild" for a while, capturing lands and defeating the Allies, but now the tide had turned. From this point on, the

Japanese would find themselves constantly on the defensive, running away from the Allies and being pushed farther and farther out of the Pacific and back toward Japan.

Over in Europe, the Germans found themselves in a similar position. After the victory in Stalingrad, the Soviets began pushing German troops farther west, out of the Soviet Union and back toward Germany. At the same time, the American and British troops were working their way up from the south. German military leaders began to sense a darkness closing in around them, and more and more often they talked quietly about the possibility of losing the war. Though Hitler refused to acknowledge it, many Germans felt that now that the United States had been drawn into the war, there was no way the Nazis could win.

"Germany will either be a world power or will not be at all!" Hitler shouted. He believed that if Germany could not win this war, then Germany did not even deserve to exist. And he felt there could be no greater shame than losing to those who were not part of what he thought of as the master race. Now, as the Allies began pushing the Nazis back, Hitler became increasingly frantic, angry—and dangerous.

"Six thousand a day," Hitler ordered Heinrich Himmler, his Chief of the Gestapo (German secret police). Himmler was instructed to tell all the Jewish ghetto and concentration camp police chiefs to round up at least 6,000 Jews every day to be sent to the death camps. Time was running out. Hitler became more and more worried about the world discovering his Final Solution plans before he could carry them out. Additionally, he was concerned about the Allies discovering the ghettos and the camps.

For some time, the Nazis had used both phony ghettos and phony concentration camps to hide their horrific treatment of Jews from the German people. German media and Red Cross representatives were invited to tour a small section of a ghetto or a camp. In those fake sections, the Nazis had actually set up imitation cafés, banks, stores, and even art galleries in an attempt to show how well Jews were being treated "while they waited for resettlement." On the days that the Red Cross and media visited, several hundred Jews were brought in from the real parts of the camps and were forced to pretend that they were happy. Tea was served, bands played, and the media would make their reports: "There is no need to worry about the Jews," one Berlin paper announced. "They live very pleasant lives within the camps, complete with fine art and tea houses."

Hitler knew, however, that this lie would be revealed as the Allies pushed into Poland. Therefore, the camps and ghettos must be emptied and destroyed. The killing must be speeded up and completed. Then everything must be reduced to ashes. No trace, Hitler insisted, could be left behind.

CHAPTER 13

The use of bombs in war was not new; bombs had been used in World War I. However, they had not been a primary weapon. World War I had still been fought mostly on the ground and in the trenches, using guns and grenades. But bombs had been used just enough to terrify people. Horrible visions of massive bombs that could destroy a city's buildings and kill its citizens haunted many people's imaginations. And many military experts predicted that World War II would be won by bombers, not by ground forces.

It was for this reason that in the spring of 1943, brand new bombers from the United States were flying into Allied bases in Africa and Great Britain every day. And by summer, hundreds of these planes were sent out on "strategic bombing" missions over Germany. These missions had specific strategies. Some bombings were meant to destroy industries and resources necessary for German warfare and everyday life. Other attacks, similar to Germany's bombing of London, were meant to terrorize the German people and destroy the German morale.

Oil fields, military bases, and industries were targeted at first, mostly during nighttime raids. These were highly successful, but American pilots grew frustrated with their inability to accurately hit all their targets in the dark. Believing that they could out-maneuver German pilots, the Americans switched to daytime raids. This was a big mistake. One after another, American planes were shot down by the more experienced German pilots.

Switching back to nighttime bombing, the American and British air forces then launched the type of devastating bombing raids that people had feared and had seen in their nightmares. From July 24 to August 3, 1943, the Allies dropped high explosive, incendiary, and phosphorus bombs on Hamburg, Germany's second-largest city. Phosphorous bombs were newly developed and particularly gruesome. Showers of the element phosphorous rained down on the residents of Hamburg, sticking to them and burning their skin. Hundreds of people jumped into the Alster River to stop the burning, only to find that the phosphorus reactivated as soon as it was exposed to oxygen and burst into flames again. Ultimately, these victims had to choose whether to die from drowning or from the flaming chemical.

Most terrifying of all was the firestorm in Hamburg on July 27. So many fires had been started by the bombings that a monstrous tornado of heat roared through the city with winds up to

150 miles an hour. It sucked out oxygen, suffocating thousands, and it superheated everything, turning an eight-square-mile area into a pit of blue-hot flame. Fires of 1,500 degrees Fahrenheit reached a height of more than 1,000 feet. By the time the raids ended and the fires were out, 50,000 residents of Hamburg had been killed and another 900,000 were left homeless.

The Allies bombed twenty-five cities throughout Germany, destroying, on average, 55 percent of a city and killing, in total, nearly half a million civilians. As for the Allies, 40,000 planes were destroyed in the process, and 160,000 airmen were killed. Was it all worth it? That's a question that is still debated today. Many people felt, and continue to feel, that such widespread slaughter of innocent German civilians was not necessary and that, in the end, these bombings had little to do with actually winning the war. Some even believed that these raids should be considered war crimes.

Adolf Hitler still refused to admit that Germany was beginning its long downward spiral toward defeat. Although his generals pointed out that the military now needed to focus on defense rather than on new attacks, Hitler turned a deaf ear to such suggestions. Switching to defense, Hitler felt, indicated fear. The Germans had developed a defensive fighter jet that could fly at more than 500 miles an hour and could possibly have chased away many of the Allied bombers as they flew toward Germany. But Hitler irritably waved off production of these jets.

"Turn them into bombers instead," he ordered, thinking only of destruction instead of protection. This was a nearly impossible task.

"One might as well have been given orders to change a horse into a cow!" one general later commented. As a result, the new jets sat unused until early 1944, when in desperation Hitler reluctantly allowed a few of the jet fighters to be flown. By then, however, it was far too late.

On the outside, Hitler remained arrogant and stubborn, but his fear was becoming more apparent to the generals who worked closely with him. More and more often, Hitler hid in the new *Führerbunker* ("shelter for the leader"), a thirty-room underground bunker with thick concrete walls. Guards stood at Hitler's door, and the entrance to the long tunnel that led to the bunker was carefully hidden. As bombs rattled and crushed Berlin, the country's leader retreated to a dimly lit room far underground and put his shaking hands over his ears.

Now completely in charge of carrying out and completing the Final Solution, Heinrich Himmler began getting quite nervous. Many of the top generals had begun questioning the murder of the Jews. Some honestly felt that Hitler had gone too far. Others were simply afraid that, should Germany lose the war, the truth would be revealed and they would be punished. Hitler had often bragged that "the victor will never be asked if he told the truth." But now victory did not look nearly as promising as it had in the early years of the war. Himmler began scurrying to ensure that the truth would never be revealed. In late 1943, Himmler ordered all Jews in the camps closest to the Soviet border to be shot. He cruelly named the operation *Erntefest* (German for "Harvest Festival"). This would be, Himmler explained, a fall harvest of lives.

On November 3, 1943, Jews were marched out of the camps and into the nearby woods. Trucks with loudspeakers blaring German dancehall music followed the Jews. Women and children were led in one direction, and men were led in another. As they were ordered to take off all their clothing, a young woman shouted, "It seems to me that we are being led to the grave!"

This young woman would later write about what happened that day. In horrifying detail, she would describe how she and hundreds of other naked women and children were led to a huge ditch. As they approached the ditch, the music from the trucks grew louder, and Nazis with rifles grew closer.

"The graves were six feet deep and full of naked bodies," she recalled. It was at that point that she realized the music was to muffle the sound of the gunshots so that it would not reach the ears of the non-Jewish prisoners still in the camp. In groups of fifty, the women were ordered to climb into the graves and lie face down on top of the dead bodies. Then the shooting began.

The young woman was shot twice in the arm, but she was not killed. Nazi soldiers walked across the backs of the dead women looking for any sign of life. If even a finger twitched, the soldiers would shoot the victim again. Pretending to be dead, the woman lay in the pile of bodies for hours, waiting to escape. At one point, she saw high flames coming from the area where the clothes had been discarded.

"Then I feared that they might burn the dead. I shivered at the thought of being burned alive. . . . Much later I crawled out of the heaps of bodies and started running for the forest."

Years later, in 1952, the diary of this young woman would be discovered in the rubble of a death camp. Her last entry was written a year after her escape from the "Harvest Festival." Her name and how she eventually died will remain a mystery, but her chilling firsthand account of this mass murder was her parting contribution to the truth.

In one day alone, *Erntefest* claimed the lives of 40,000 Jews.

"We want this war over with. The quickest way to get it over with is to go get the bastards who started it. The quicker they are whipped, the quicker we can go home. The shortest way home is through Berlin and Tokyo. And when we get to Berlin, I am personally going to shoot that paper-hanging son-of-a-bitch Hitler. Just like I'd shoot a snake!" These were the words of the tough-talking General George C. Patton on the evening of June 5, 1944. For nearly six months, the Allies had been planning for this day. It was time to get to Berlin.

Nearly a year earlier, Roosevelt and Churchill had met to discuss the best way to launch the land invasion of German territory. After much thought and consideration, they agreed that Great Britain would be used as the base and that, once everything was ready, the Allies would cross the English Channel and land in Normandy, France. France was still heavily guarded by the Germans, so the Allies knew they must be totally prepared for battle once they landed on the beaches of Normandy.

And so the massive preparations began. Code-named "Operation Overlord," this invasion would turn nearly all of Great Britain into a gigantic temporary military base. More than three million soldiers, half of them from the United States, poured into Great Britain to train. Every month, more than 500,000 tons of supplies landed on Britain's shores, most coming from America.

Finally, it was time to go. June 5, 1944, had been chosen as "D-Day," a military term designating the beginning of an attack. However, on the evening of June 4, General Eisenhower, the decision-maker, paced in his headquarters in Great

Britain. A raging storm was pounding the shores of Normandy, making a beach landing in fewer than twelve hours nearly impossible. June 5 had been chosen because of the high tide and full moon. The tides and moonlight would be good for three days, and then the next high tide would not take place for two more weeks. Eisenhower knew that the troops were more than ready to go—delaying D-Day would frustrate the soldiers and deaden their enthusiasm. Then a report came in. There was no guarantee, but it looked as though the weather might clear up for just a few hours on June 6.

Eisenhower would take the risk. "Okay," he said quietly to his generals. "We'll go."

Five beaches along the coast of Normandy had been chosen for the landings. These beaches were code-named Omaha, Utah, Gold, Juno, and Sword, with Omaha and Utah being the landing spots for the American soldiers. Hours before troops reached these shores, about 15,000 paratroopers had been dropped through the dark skies to locations inland from the beaches, in areas guarded by the Germans. Many of these paratroopers were dropped in the wrong place, or were captured or killed by the Germans. Many others, however, under the cover of night, cut power lines, destroyed bridges, and set up defensive positions along the roads in an attempt to block any reinforcements the Germans would send once the Normandy beaches were invaded.

Next, the tremendous fleet of ships rolled across the English Channel. As land came into sight, the Allies' battleships opened fire on the Germans. Then came the transports with the Allied soldiers. It was the largest water-to-land invasion of all time, attempting to transfer more than 150,000 troops ashore. Barbed wire, massive concrete forts and machine gun nests, and steel beam "tank traps" greeted the soldiers. The wind howled, and tall waves crashed. On Omaha Beach, rockets, grenades, and machine-gun fire from the Germans killed hundreds of men before they even reached the shore. Soldiers had to wade through dead bodies and debris. Those who made it ashore were forced to crawl on all fours with their heads down in an attempt to dodge bullets. Before long, Omaha Beach was covered with the dead bodies of American soldiers.

The generals in charge worried. Perhaps this plan had been a mistake. Maybe the men should return to the ships and retreat. But the plans for this invasion had been so complex and time-consuming that the generals were reluctant to retreat. The orders to continue bringing troops ashore went forth, and the gruesome battle continued until nightfall.

Then good news reached the generals.

By sheer determination and unfailing bravery, the soldiers had managed to move through enemy fire and were now opening the way for the armored tanks. Tanks rolled by the hundreds onto the beaches of Normandy and thundered past enemy forces to the roads. The German guns and blockades could do nothing to stop these metal monsters.

"Success!" the generals shouted. But the success had come at a serious cost. More than 4,000 Allied soldiers lay dead in the water or on the beaches of Normandy. Still, the invasion had caught the Germans by surprise, and the generals estimated that if D-Day had been postponed and the Germans had caught on to the Allies' plans, the death toll could have reached 75,000.

"I thank the gods of war that we went when we did," Eisenhower later remarked.

In the Soviet Union, Joseph Stalin could not have been more pleased with the success of the D-Day invasion. Soviet troops were continuing to push the Germans westward, and now the Americans and British would begin pushing them eastward. It would be, Stalin hoped, the classic military trap—in time, the Germans would find themselves with the enemy on both sides, leaving them nowhere to run.

Now it was time for the Allies to move across France. Parts of France had been occupied by the Germans for four years, but the Allied forces far outnumbered the pockets of German soldiers. Helping the Allies sweep through France were the mild summer weather, the open country where vehicles could move quickly, and the moral support of the French people, who ran out to see the soldiers, crying tears of joy and bringing them food, wine, flowers, and even songs. Military support was added by the French Resistance, which had been fighting the Germans all along—they had been waiting years for this very moment.

"Burn Paris down to the ground!" Hitler ordered from his bunker in Berlin. "Leave nothing but ashes."

Terrified and furious over the success of the Allies, Hitler decided that if he could not have Paris, then no one would have Paris. Because the Allies had moved quickly and victoriously through France, the minimal damage to its cities had not satisfied Hitler. German cities had been devastated by Allied bombers, and now he wanted to see Paris in ruins. He was, perhaps, the only one who wanted this. Even Hitler's own generals refused to follow his orders, quietly surrendering to the Allies rather than taking revenge by destroying one of the world's most beautiful cities.

By the fall of 1944, the Allies began getting into position to invade Germany. British and American troops had moved just as quickly through the occupied areas of Holland and Belgium, and now a long Allied frontline extended for miles along the German border. Generals gathered and planned. Troops rested briefly. And then one of the worst winter storms of nearly half a century suddenly blew into Europe, taking everyone by surprise.

However, a much worse surprise came on the heels of the storm.

"I have no doubt," Hitler said confidently of this new unforeseen twist, "that *this* will end the war. Germany shall win after all."

CHAPTER 14

Hitler had fond memories of how German troops had defeated the French back in 1940 by bursting through the thick Ardennes Forest and catching the French troops completely by surprise. Now Hitler planned to use the same surprise attack on the Allies. After all, it was the middle of winter. Who in his right mind would expect an attack coming by way of a dark, snowed-in woods? This was the mind-set Hitler hoped the Allies would have, and to a great extent his hopes were fulfilled.

Just before this surprise attack, Eisenhower had been feeling uneasy. Even though it had begun to look as though there was no way Germany could win the war now that the Allies were closing in from both sides, Eisenhower warned his commanders not to give in to what he called "victory fever." They must remain on high alert, regardless of how close victory seemed. Unfortunately, the troops just west of the Ardennes were in many ways the least alert. Most of these men were either fresh recruits or soldiers who were recovering from injuries. Eisenhower had placed the weakest troops there because, as Hitler had correctly guessed, Eisenhower did not think the Germans would attempt an attack through such a difficult route at such a bad time of year.

Hitler's plan was for German troops to storm through this weak pocket, thereby breaking the line of Allied troops in half. Then the Germans would continue on, taking over the Belgian cities of Brussels and Antwerp. Most of the Allies' supplies came through those cities, and if the Germans could seize them, the Allies would have great difficulty. Stranded along the German border without food or supplies in the middle of a terrible winter, the Allies were sure to surrender. Hitler was so confident of this plan that he committed nearly all of his remaining troops and artillery to it.

Hitler's commanders, however, thought this last-ditch effort was crazy.

"All he wants me to do is cross a river, capture Brussels, and then go and take Antwerp," one commander said sarcastically. "And all this in the worst time of year . . . where the snow is waist deep . . . with divisions made up chiefly of kids and sick old men—and all this at Christmas!"

Even so, at first the attack was a success for the Germans. The Allies were caught totally by surprise as the German panzers once again came roaring out of the Ardennes on December 16, 1944. The tanks literally rolled over the camps, smashing everything in sight into the deep snow. For the next few days, the Germans rolled on, pushing the Allies back and creating a bulge of German forces in the long Allied line. For this reason, this battle was named "the Battle of the Bulge."

The Allies were tremendously outnumbered and overpowered where the Germans attacked, and for a short time it looked as if Hitler's unusual plan might work. However, before the Germans could completely break through, the Allied troops rushed in from both directions with much more speed than the Germans had anticipated. Next, the German tanks began running out of fuel as they were slowed down by the Allies. And then on December 23, the winter storm suddenly and unexpectedly cleared. The skies were wide open for the Allied air forces, something Hitler had not counted on.

The German tanks and troops were now sitting ducks. Their only means of supply were horse-drawn wagons, and these were quickly destroyed or blocked. In the battle, which lasted about five weeks, Germany suffered more than 100,000 casualties and lost about 700 tanks. Hitler's final gamble had not paid off, but his last-gasp effort had been terribly deadly for the Allied forces, too. The Americans suffered more than 80,000 casualties, making the Battle of the Bulge the deadliest battle of World War II for the Americans.

However, the Allies had closed the bulge, and in doing so had closed the door on any chance of the Germans winning the war in Europe. Now all that remained was the final push into Berlin and the march right to Hitler's door. But that sweet moment of victory would not happen in the way that many of the Allies had imagined. Eisenhower, as Supreme Allied Commander, had decided to let the Soviets have the satisfaction of wrapping things up. Many Americans were angry with Eisenhower for deciding to hold American troops back from Berlin: Why shouldn't *we* be the ones to get the glory after all we've done and sacrificed? Wasn't it our own General Patton who had been chomping at the bit to shoot Hitler like he would a snake?

However, it had also been the straight-talking Patton who had once pointed out, "If everyone is thinking alike, someone isn't thinking." And now Eisenhower thought differently about the invasion of Berlin. He wisely saw that it was more important, both symbolically and emotionally, for a European power to crush Berlin than for the Americans to do so. As for "sacrifice," the Soviets had, by far, sacrificed the most, in terms of both human life and land.

And so as the brutal winter of 1944 began to draw to a close, the Soviets moved westward. As they made their way, they came across the Nazi death camp at Auschwitz, and the horrors that met the eyes of the Soviet soldiers and generals only added more fuel to their raging hatred of the Germans. The Soviets were now determined to crush Berlin, showing no mercy for anyone or anything. They had assembled the largest military force in European history for this final act, and as it rumbled and thundered toward Germany's capital, millions of German citizens did the only thing they could do: They ran for their lives.

Before the Soviets had come across the survivors remaining at Auschwitz, the Nazis had made one last frenzied dash to empty the death camps of prisoners and to destroy any evidence of the crimes they had committed. Guards ran through the camps in the middle of the night screaming for the prisoners to come out of the barracks. As the terrified prisoners stumbled out, they were shot by the hundreds and thrown into hastily dug pits or burned in giant bonfires.

Some prisoners hid in the camp buildings, but they were forced out when the guards doused the buildings with gasoline and set them on fire. In desperation, some prisoners sought any hiding places that could not burn. A prisoner at Birkenau recalled his life-saving decision:

"My friends and I hid in the lavatories, peeking through the doors. But we knew they would burn the lavatories, too. So we jumped through the toilet seats and into the pit of excrement. And this was the worst experience of my life. For several hours we stood there, chest deep in human waste. Not a word, barely breathing. Then there was absolute silence for a very long time, then the sound of the huge gate opening. And, oh God, the sweetest sound—the Russian language! Liberation had arrived."

Many thousands of other prisoners were not so lucky. After shooting as many Jews as possible, the guards gathered the rest and led them on what would become known as the Death Marches. For days, sometimes for a hundred miles or more, the prisoners were forced to walk in freezing weather with no food. Guards ripped blankets from their hands and sprayed them with water just to watch the ice form on their skin. Those who complained or fell behind were shot. Soon, bodies lined the roadside ditches for miles.

Prisoners were never told where they were headed. Himmler had sent out vague orders to get the last of the Jews to remote locations in Germany where they could be disposed of secretly. However, the hope was that most of them would die on the way. After marching many miles, prisoners were crammed once again into cattle cars and sent off on an endless journey.

"We were given no food," recalled the former Auschwitz prisoner Elie Wiesel. "We lived on snow; it took the place of bread. The days were like nights. . . . The train was traveling slowly, often stopping for several hours and then setting off again. . . . We were no more than frozen bodies. Our eyes closed, we waited merely for the next stop, so that we could unload our dead."

As the marches and cattle carloads made their way through the small German towns, many people turned their backs on these suffering, starving people in rags. Hard as it is to imagine, they refused to help even with a crust of bread or an old coat. However, there were other Germans who were stunned and heartbroken by what they saw. Some risked their own lives to sneak food or blankets to the prisoners. Others whisked groups of prisoners out of the long lines when guards weren't watching and led them to safety. A German Catholic named Oskar Schindler tricked Nazi guards at one railway station into believing that a cattle car packed with Jews was actually a load of supplies for his ammunition factory. The car was redirected, and Schindler managed to save all but sixteen prisoners aboard.

These long columns of prisoners in the Death Marches were often barely more than a day ahead of the Soviet forces moving in from the east or the American and British forces moving in from the west.

"In such a way," one survivor sadly remembered, "there were thousands who had endured camp life who, at the last minute, were murdered a moment before liberation."

And as the Allied forces closed in, many Nazi guards knew the fate that awaited them. Some were plainly afraid. Others had begun to regret their actions, realizing too late just how evil the Holocaust really was. One guard who had participated in forcing nearly 10,000 Jews over a cliff into the Baltic Sea wrote at that time: "It is terrible that Germans were capable of such a thing. . . . If the Russians march in, which is only a question of days or weeks now, they will do the same to us as we have done to the Jews. A German will dangle from every tree. The forest will be full of German corpses!"

It was perhaps this combination of fear, guilt, and hopelessness that led German commanders all along the German border to surrender to the Allies in April 1945. This was in direct defiance of Hitler's orders to never surrender.

When Hitler heard of the surrender, he screamed that this was "the most shameful betrayal in human history." In particular, Hitler was furious with Himmler, who, Hitler reminded anyone still listening, had often said, "My honor is my loyalty." Now all loyalty was dead.

Hitler now stayed locked away, deep in the dark rooms of his underground bunker for twenty-four hours a day—pacing, shouting, and completely losing his grip on reality. All that remained was Berlin, and though the Germans had no hope of defeating the approaching monstrous Soviet army, Hitler insisted they fight.

"To the last man and the last shot," were Hitler's exact orders. Furthermore, even citizens of Berlin were not allowed to leave the city. Hitler was less worried about Berliners being slaughtered than he was about his own reputation if Berlin also surrendered. And since all of Hitler's best generals had been wise enough to give up the fight, Hitler appointed Joseph Goebbels as the military leader of Berlin's defense. This made matters much worse. Goebbels may have been a master of spreading lies and inventing propaganda, but he had no skill as a military leader.

Goebbels took on the position with pride, however. He was one of very few people who remained loyal to the Führer until the end. His loyalty often overlapped into an obsession with Hitler, but this may have had more to do with Goebbels's desire for power rather than with honest admiration for Hitler. In any event, his loyalty paid off—if only briefly. As the rumble of Soviet tanks shook Berlin, Goebbels was the second most powerful man in Germany.

"Fight with everything you have got!" he shouted to the ragtag army of crippled soldiers, old men, and boys. "The battle for Berlin must become the signal for the whole nation to rise up in battle!"

But it was far too late for that. The battle raged for nine days as the Soviets went, literally, street by street and building by building, destroying everything and everyone in their path. On the afternoon of May 2, the Soviet flag replaced the German flag in the center of Berlin. And then, finally, Soviet footsteps approached Hitler's bunker. But if the soldiers had been hoping to find Hitler cowering, they were disappointed.

Only hours earlier, Hitler, along with Eva Braun, his longtime mistress whom he had married the day before, had retired to a private room. There in the darkness, as the walls of the bunker rattled from the fighting above, Hitler handed Eva a capsule of poison, which she obediently took. Then the man who had been the mastermind of unimaginable evil, the vain leader who had sworn that his Nazi government would last one thousand years, put a gun to his head and shot a bullet into his brain.

By the time the Soviets arrived, Hitler's and Braun's bodies had been burned and the remains hidden. Joseph Goebbels, whom Hitler had appointed Chancellor just before his death, expressed sorrow that "such a great man is no longer with us." The next day Goebbels's wife saw to the death of their six children, and then Goebbels and his wife took their own lives. Neither Hitler nor Goebbels in his final days expressed even a word of regret or remorse for his part in the murder of millions of Jews and other "non-perfect" people. In fact, Hitler's very last words in his will asked the people of Germany to "resist mercilessly the poisoner of all nations"—the Jews.

"It's over! It's over!"

These words were chanted on May 8, 1945, by the half million people who jammed Times Square in New York City. May 8 had been declared Victory in Europe Day, or V-E Day. Confetti fell through the air, and bands played. In Moscow, nearly three million Soviets cheered, cried, and danced. In London, Princess Elizabeth stepped outside of Buckingham Palace to greet the crowds for the first time in six years.

However, there was great sorrow mixed with the celebration. In the United States, President Roosevelt, who had been ill for some time, had died just a few weeks before the war in Europe was won. The day after his death, his name had been placed at the top of the war casualty list published in papers across the country. Many Americans felt that Roosevelt had given his life to this great battle in the same way that millions of soldiers had.

In the Soviet Union, towns and cities lay in ruins. An astounding twenty-four million Soviet people had died. Everyone celebrating in Red Square in Moscow on V-E Day had personally known someone who had died on the battlefields, in the destroyed cities, or in the Nazi camps.

And millions of "displaced persons," as the military called them, moved throughout Europe, trying to return to the homes they had been forced from during the war. Among those displaced persons were the survivors of the Holocaust. Their unspeakable joy over finally being liberated from the grip of the Nazi death machine was always clouded with sorrow and pain. Many survivors were alone, having lost all their relatives and friends. Most were still recovering from illness, starvation, and years of physical abuse. All were without any money or belongings.

And strange as it may sound, many survivors felt a sense of guilt for having survived. It is estimated that the Nazis murdered close to twelve million of those they considered to be less than human. This included Jews, Poles, Soviets, homosexuals, Jehovah's Witnesses, gypsies, and the physically and mentally disabled. Now, as those who had been freed walked through the springtime air and heard the shouts of joy, many could not help but wonder, "Why me? Why did I live when so many died?"

Still, the celebrations resounded across the United States and Europe. It had been a long, bitter battle, and now it was over, right?

Wrong.

Always happy to offer a reality check when one was needed, Winston Churchill addressed his country and the world on the evening of May 8.

"The evildoers . . . are now prostrate before us. . . . But let us not forget for a moment the toils and efforts that lie ahead. Japan, with all her treachery and greed, remains unsubdued."

CHAPTER 15

Although for much of 1944 the focus had been on the war in Europe, American forces in the Pacific had been busy, too. Island by island, the Allies moved closer and closer to Japan. This strategy was known as "island hopping." Some islands that were heavily guarded by the Japanese were passed over. The main goal was to keep hopping islands until the Allies were sitting on Japan's doorstep. This made the Japanese very nervous, because as the Allies took over islands and set up new bases, their bombers were soon within striking distance of Japan.

Remaining true to his promise of "I shall return," General MacArthur had indeed returned. He led troops as they secured New Guinea, and as a top commander of the Allied forces, he oversaw the taking of Saipan, Tinian, and Guam. All of these islands were stepping stones to the Philippines, where MacArthur had endured defeat two years earlier. He vowed that he would not be defeated again.

The Philippine people had suffered terribly during the years of the Japanese occupation. Like the Nazis when they had occupied other countries, the Japanese threw people out of their homes, stole and destroyed property, and raped and killed as a way of reminding the Filipinos who was in power. Additionally, they forced a large part of the population into slave labor, often working men, women, and children to death.

The second battle for the Philippines raged from October 20, 1944 to September 2, 1945. The fighting was particularly brutal and deadly. Japan had now begun using *kamikaze* (Japanese for "divine wind") pilots in an all-out attempt to regain the upper hand in battle. These pilots loaded their planes with bombs and explosives, but instead of dropping the bombs *on* their targets, they flew directly *into* their targets. In particular, the kamikaze attacks focused on large warships such as battleships and aircraft carriers. So devoted to their country were these young kamikaze pilots that they considered sacrificing their lives the greatest honor of all. As a result, there was never a shortage of pilots eagerly requesting kamikaze missions.

These suicidal missions were nearly impossible to predict or stop. The planes would come screaming in at such great speeds that the anti-aircraft guns were practically useless. They terrorized the Allies and cost the lives of hundreds of American soldiers. Even so, the Japanese could not hold back the

Americans this time around. By early 1945, the Japanese forces were beginning to run out of both firepower and manpower—just as the Allies, having won the war in Europe, were greatly increasing both. MacArthur's return was victorious.

Now the Allies took aim at two small islands that were part of Japan. The country of Japan was actually made up of about 7,000 islands, stretching from the Soviet Union to South Korea. Many of these islands were very small, and some were even uninhabited. But two of them, Iwo Jima and Okinawa, were important to the Allies. Capturing these two islands would put the Allies only a few hundred miles away from Tokyo, the very heart of Japan's power.

In many ways, the battles of Iwo Jima and Okinawa were decided before they even began. There was really no hope for the Japanese to overpower the Allies—but this didn't mean that the Japanese would not fight to the bitter end. On Iwo Jima, many of Japan's 18,000 defenders hid in caves, holes, and concrete bunkers. Marines literally went from hole to hole, forcing the Japanese out with explosives, until the Japanese forces were reduced by half. Still, the Japanese would not surrender. They were crushed to 5,000, yet they fought on. Even when only 1,000 Japanese soldiers were left, they showed no fear and no sign of retreat. If captured, they killed themselves rather than allow the enemy to take them. By the end, only 200 shamed and raving

Japanese soldiers were taken prisoner—17,800 had preferred death.

This same scene played out on Okinawa. Here, when the Japanese realized they could not win, thousands threw themselves over the steep rocky cliffs to their deaths. Literally hundreds of kamikaze pilots filled the air and crashed into American ships, killing thousands of Allied sailors. In the end, the Allies, as expected, were victorious, but the absolute fearlessness and relentlessness of the Japanese were troubling. The Allies had never seen anything like it.

The day after Roosevelt had suddenly died, the new President, Harry S. Truman, stood before the press corps and shook his head.

"Boys," he said, "if you ever pray, pray for me now. I don't know whether you fellows ever had a load of hay fall on you, but when they told me yesterday what had happened, I felt like the moon, the stars, and all the planets had fallen on me."

It was now up to a brand-new President to lead his country to final victory in World War II. Truman was a straightforward leader who was not afraid to take necessary action. At the same time, he was a compassionate man, whose heart broke when he considered the terrible toll on human life this war was taking. Like millions of people worldwide, he just wanted World War II to come to an end. And now, just when it seemed that the Japanese, who were far outnumbered and were losing every battle, would certainly surrender, an odd thing happened: They began fighting even harder.

Heavy B-29 bombers were now attacking Japan daily. Japanese civilians had no bomb shelters and nowhere to run. When the bombs fell, thousands died. In Tokyo, a monstrous firestorm swept through the crowded city when nearly 1,700 tons of incendiary bombs were dropped in a single night. More than 100,000 people died in that attack.

The Japanese military's only response to this was to train old men, women, and children (all the young men were either fighting or dead) how to use sharpened bamboo poles to kill the enemy. A land invasion had not happened yet, but when it did, the military encouraged civilians to spear as many Allied soldiers as possible. They were then fiercely instructed to kill themselves before allowing the enemy to capture them.

Insane. Fanatical. Crazy. These were the words many in the United States military used to describe the extreme measures of the Japanese. Why didn't they just give up? As the spring of 1945 turned to summer, there was no doubt that the Japanese had been defeated. Even the Japanese military had conducted a secret study to determine whether its fate could be turned around, and it had concluded that it could not—Japan had clearly lost the war.

And yet the Japanese fought on with ever-increasing viciousness. The more hopeless things got for the Japanese, the deadlier they became in battles. It defied all reason. Or did it? Amazingly, in its many-thousand-year history, the country of Japan had never been defeated in war. It was believed by some, including a former American ambassador to Japan, that Japanese culture simply could not comprehend the idea of surrender. To the Japanese, the only option was to continue fighting, even if that meant fighting to the very last person.

With this in mind, President Truman had some very difficult decisions to make. The bombing raids didn't seem to be making much of a difference. The Japanese seemed willing to accept that cities would be damaged and people would die. In the meantime, the constant raids were taking a toll on the Allies—how long would they have to continue? Truman decided that it was time to begin planning the invasion of Japan. An actual takeover of the country would certainly force the Japanese to surrender. There was perhaps no one more excited about launching a land invasion than General MacArthur. He, like many, had been disappointed when the Americans were held back from invading and forcing surrender in Berlin. Now the Americans would get the glory in Japan.

However, there was a dark side to this plan. It meant more war, perhaps years more, and it meant many more Allied deaths. Some predicted that close to half a million soldiers would be killed or wounded. And as eager as MacArthur was to get going, he bluntly disagreed with these predictions.

"More like one million," he corrected. "And most of them Americans."

Then in the midst of all this, another even darker option for bringing an end to the war entered the discussion: using an atomic bomb. Even before World War II had begun, American scientists had been working on the bomb. It was no secret that the Germans were also studying the use of nuclear fission to create a monstrous bomb. If they created it first, the rest of the world would be at their mercy. Many American scientists, including Albert Einstein, who had escaped from Germany, had urged President Roosevelt to approve development of the bomb. Approval had been given, and the project to build the bomb, named "the Manhattan Project," was started in 1942.

By 1945, the atomic bomb had been created at the giant nuclear weapons plant in Oak Ridge, Tennessee. Scientists then gathered at a desolate desert location in New Mexico on July 16, 1945, to test their creation. In the early morning, before daylight, the bomb was detonated. Scientists and military officials watched from more than ten miles away.

"The whole country was lighted by a searing light with the intensity many times that of the midday sun," one observer recalled. "It was golden, purple, violet, gray, and blue. It lighted every peak, crevasse, and ridge of the nearby mountain range with a clarity and beauty that cannot be described but must be seen to be imagined."

J. Robert Oppenheimer was the scientist in charge of overseeing the development of this terrible weapon. Nicknamed "the Father of the Atomic Bomb," Oppenheimer knew what had been created, and he saw no beauty in it.

"We knew the world would not be the same," he later said. "A few people laughed, a few people cried, most people were silent."

And as Oppenheimer witnessed the massive burning ball that shook the earth and rose into the sky, the words from a Hindu scripture echoed in his head: "Now I am become Death, the destroyer of worlds."

News of the successful test of the atom bomb was rushed to President Truman. Now he and Churchill had to decide whether to use this powerful new weapon. The decision, however, Truman would later explain, "was no great decision. . . . It was purely a military decision." In other words, both he and Churchill knew they would have to use the bomb to force Japan's surrender.

"There was unanimous, automatic, unquestioned agreement," Churchill said.

This did not mean that Truman did not personally struggle with using such a destructive weapon. Just two weeks before the bomb would be dropped on Japan, Truman wrote in his diary: "We have discovered the most terrible bomb in the history of the world. It may be the fire destruction prophesied in the Euphrates Valley Era, after Noah and his fabulous Ark."

On August 6, 1945, an atomic bomb nicknamed "Little Boy" headed toward the Japanese industrial city of Hiroshima aboard a B-29 bomber. Hiroshima was chosen because it was a military manufacturing center and because it had never been bombed before. A previously untouched target would allow analysts to gauge just how much damage an atomic bomb would really do. Likewise, it would clearly show the Japanese how terrible this new weapon was.

The residents of Hiroshima received no warning. As the Japanese civilians went about their regular morning activities, an explosion unlike any explosion ever witnessed on the face of the earth reduced a bustling city to a barren wasteland.

"The morning was still, the place was cool and pleasant," recalled one witness who had been far enough away to survive the bombing. "Then a tremendous flash of light cut across the sky. . . . It seemed like a sheet of sun."

The mushroom cloud from Little Boy rose eleven miles into the sky. It was estimated that more than 70,000 people were killed instantly, many of them leaving nothing more than a shadow of dust in the outline of their bodies. Many thousands more died later from injuries and diseases resulting from radiation. One reporter described Hiroshima as he walked around one day after the blast: "Everything that burns was burnt. . . . The whole city became extinct."

And still Japan would not surrender.

As a result, three days later a much larger atomic bomb, dubbed "Fat Man," was dropped on the big port city of Nagasaki. The mountains surrounding Nagasaki blocked some of the wall of roaring fire from the bomb, but, again, about 70,000 people were killed immediately, and nearly a third of the city was leveled.

Japan's Emperor Hirohito had finally had enough. Although people in the Japanese military still refused to accept surrender, Hirohito insisted that they must. In a speech to the Japanese people, Hirohito explained the grim reality of foolishly continuing this losing battle:

"Should we continue to fight, it would not only result in an ultimate collapse and obliteration of the Japanese nation, but also it would lead to the total extinction of human civilization."

Hirohito clearly saw, as did many others, that the use of nuclear bombs was a far greater danger than anyone could have ever imagined. These were not just the type of weapons that could end the war—they could end the world. Since that terrible week in August of 1945, nuclear weapons have never been used again. Still, many people argue that the use of the atomic bomb as a way of forcing

Japan's surrender was both cruel and unnecessary. Even General Dwight Eisenhower, still wrapping things up in Europe, shook his head angrily when he was told about the bombings.

"The Japanese were ready to surrender," he argued. "It wasn't necessary to hit them with that awful thing."

Two weeks later, on September 2, 1945, representatives of the Empire of Japan boarded a United States battleship anchored near Tokyo. The Allies had chosen a battleship to be the site of the surrender ceremony because they feared that the Japanese military, still angry about admitting defeat, might spring a surprise attack if the meeting took place in Tokyo. In the end, however, the military was as faithful to its emperor's orders as it had been to the battle. The terms of surrender were signed peacefully.

As the ceremony drew to a close, General MacArthur stood and turned to the military leaders gathered there. He looked into their war-weary and worried faces and spoke quietly:

"It is . . . the hope of all mankind that from this solemn occasion a better world shall emerge out of the blood and carnage of the past . . . a world dedicated to the dignity of man and the fulfillment of his most cherished wish—for freedom, tolerance, and justice."

After six long years, World War II had finally come to an end.

EPILOGUE

The Aftermath of World War II

Americans could not wait to celebrate Victory over Japan Day (V-J Day). As soon as the second atomic bomb was dropped and Japan's officials were barely beginning to put the official surrender into writing, New York's Times Square was packed with people. Old newspapers full of bad news were torn up and dropped like confetti from the windows of tall office buildings; bands played; total strangers hugged and kissed. Although the official V-J Day would not come until August 14, 1945, crowds around the world celebrated in the days and months leading up to it.

"At last the job is finished," Winston Churchill was reported to have said as he lit one of his trademark cigars in celebration.

And what a job it had been. The entire world was quite a different place in 1945 than it had been in 1939. There was much to celebrate, but there was certainly as much, if not more, to mourn. The facts and numbers from World War II are impossible to even begin to imagine. Between 65 and 80 million people died, including close to 12 million slaughtered by the Nazis in their crazed attempt to create their master race in Germany. Of these 12 million, 6 million were Jews. It is estimated that more than one third of the world's Jewish population died during the Holocaust. World War II was, by far, the deadliest war ever to have been fought.

With the exception of the United States, every country that had been involved in the war was bankrupt and in tatters. Entire cities had been leveled; cultural treasures had been reduced to dust; thousands of miles of roadways and railways had been blown up; and countless bridges, canals, and dams had been wiped out. One displaced person who had returned to his home in Poland after the war summed it up by saying, "I look around and recognize nothing. The faces I see on these ruined streets—I recognize no one. My home is gone. My people are gone. I feel as though I am a ghost drifting through, like I am barely here myself."

In addition to the war's death and destruction, the end of the war brought what was known as an "uneasy peace." General MacArthur and others may have hoped for a new world that would have learned from the horrors of World War II and dedicated itself to "freedom, tolerance, and justice," but this was not always the case:

In Asia, the British and French wrongly assumed that they could just return to their old colonies and enforce their European rule again. Natives who were tired of outsiders telling them what to do fought back viciously, often using weapons the Japanese had left behind.

In Palestine, tempers flared. Many Jews returned to their ancestral homeland, where they hoped they would finally find safety. However, they were met by angry Palestinian Arabs who didn't want them there.

In China, with the fear of Japanese takeover now removed, civil war between Nationalists and Communists started up again.

And in Europe, Stalin returned to his tyrannical ways, refusing to allow displaced persons to leave the Soviet Union and instead forcing them into slave labor to help rebuild his country. Furthermore, Stalin pushed Poles out of Poland and into Germany. Germany had been occupied by the Allies, with eastern Germany designated as the Soviet zone. Now Stalin set his sights on clearly dividing Europe, with the Communist Soviets dominating the east. The farther west he could push the Polish people, the better. Although Stalin had cooperated with democratic nations during the war, he was no longer interested in being friendly with countries that were not Communist.

Winston Churchill watched what was happening in postwar Europe with dismay.

"A shadow has fallen upon the scenes so lately lighted by the Allied victory," he said less than a year after V-E Day. "An iron curtain has descended across the Continent. . . . This is certainly not the Liberated Europe we fought to build up. Nor is it one which contains the essentials of permanent peace."

It was this "Iron Curtain" that would continue to build tension between former allies, particularly between the Soviet Union and the United States. Suspicious and worried about the United States' nuclear weapons, the Soviets began creating nuclear weapons of their own. In response, the United States added to its nuclear arsenal. This competition to have the most weapons led to what became known as "the arms race."

For nearly forty years, both countries kept a nervous eye on each other, preparing for war but never declaring it. This period was known as "the Cold War." It was "cold" because none of the nuclear weapons created were ever used (much to the relief of the entire world), but icy hatred and hostility between Soviets and Americans continued for years.

Despite the ongoing and newly created problems around the world following World War II, the Allies' victory was a very proud achievement. Many consider it to be the greatest war triumph of all time. Still, it should be remembered that even the most famous generals of World War II were no fans of war. In his farewell address delivered to a joint session of Congress, General MacArthur said,

"I know war as few other men now living know it, and nothing to me is more revolting. I have long advocated its complete abolition, as its very destructiveness on both friend and foe has rendered it useless as a method of settling international disputes."

And not long before he died, Franklin Roosevelt expressed his feelings about war: "I have seen war. I have seen war on land and sea. I have seen blood running from the wounded. . . . I have seen the dead in the mud. I have seen cities destroyed. . . . I have seen children starving. I have seen the agony of mothers and wives. I hate war."

World War II was no exception. It did little, as MacArthur pointed out, to "settle international disputes." In fact, in the war's aftermath many countries and people were left destroyed and bitter. And as Roosevelt observed, it was, like every war, a nightmare of death, agony, and starvation.

What, then, made World War II different?

In a word: Hitler. While many wars are fought over land, money, oil, or conflicting religious and political beliefs, World War II, to a great extent, was fought to end the murderous work of a mad dictator. Much of the world worked together and put aside differences for several years in order to stop what many agreed was nothing less than pure evil.

"Never before," wrote a German historian after the war, "had any state, with all the authority of its responsible leader, decided and announced that it intended to kill off a particular group of human beings, including the old, the women, the children, and the infants, as completely as possible."

Certainly, there have been cruel and bloodthirsty leaders throughout the history of the world. And there have been many groups of people who have been targeted for persecution or worse. But there had never been a plan like that of the Nazis to secretly and systematically slaughter an entire group of people simply for the sake of killing them.

"What luck for the rulers that men do not think," Hitler was often quoted as smugly saying. However, in the case of World War II, men (and women) *did* think. And they agreed, worldwide, that what the Nazis were doing must be stopped—at any cost. For this reason, the terrible sacrifices that millions made during World War II stand out as some of the most admirable in the history of war. World War II was a war fought mainly to overcome evil, as opposed to a war fought for personal gain.

"I have never personally hated the Jews. . . . But Himmler had ordered it and had even explained the necessity, and I really never gave much thought to whether it was wrong."

That was the defense argument of Rudolf Hess, the Nazi commander of Auschwitz, who admitted to overseeing the murder of 2.5 million Jews. In the winter of 1945, Hess and twenty-one other former Nazi leaders were captured and put on trial in Nuremberg, Germany, accused of committing war crimes. A few men were acquitted, but the rest were sentenced either to life in prison or to death by hanging.

The main target of these trials was Hermann Goering, the vain commander of the Luftwaffe and Hitler's right-hand man during the final days of fighting in the Soviet Union. Goering claimed that he had tried to restrain those who were taking actions against the Jews, that he had not known about the mass extermination, and that he had wanted only to build a stronger Germany.

But the judge didn't buy it. Goering's actions over the previous two decades had made his position crystal clear.

"Goering's guilt is unique in its enormity," the judge declared. "The record discloses no excuses for this man."

Afraid of the pain of being hanged, Goering requested that he be "shot as a soldier instead of hanged like a common criminal." The court immediately denied his request. Why should a man who had killed so many get to choose his own means of death? In desperation, Goering found a way to obtain two poison capsules. In the end, this Supreme Commander, a bully and a monster feared by millions, chose to take his own life.

On the other side of the world, similar trials for Japanese war criminals took place in Tokyo from May 1946 to November 1948. As at the Nuremberg trials, only the highest-ranking and most important military leaders were tried. But in an unusual form of justice, more than 4,400 Japanese leaders and soldiers were tried in the countries of their victims and were convicted of war crimes. Many were sent to work prisons, and about 1,000 were executed.

After helping to liberate Jewish prisoners in Dachau, a Nazi concentration camp in Germany, a group of U.S. military officers were led on an inspection of the execution grounds of the camp. The Nazis had fled only days earlier—they had been in the hurried midst of trying to kill the last of the prisoners before the Allies arrived.

Now, Jewish prisoners, who had been forced to assist in the murders, led the American soldiers through the death factory. In one large warehouse, 4,000 bodies were stacked nearly to the ceiling. The smell and sight was so overwhelming that it made the soldiers physically ill. Next, the soldiers were led to the long rows of ovens where bodies had been burned. Some of the ovens were still filled with bones and ash. Finally, one of the prisoners pointed to mounds of ashes outside. Surrounding the mounds were rakes and wheelbarrows and gardening tools. The Nazis had used the ashes of their victims as fertilizer for their flower and vegetable gardens.

"No wonder their flowers were so beautiful," one officer observed.

After witnessing these things, a young American lieutenant named William Cowling wrote a letter to his parents. He felt it was important to tell them the truth about what he had seen. "When I tell you [this story]," he wrote, "you probably won't believe all the details. I knew when I heard such stories back in the States I never believed them and now even after seeing them with my own eyes, it is hard for me to believe it."

It was this inability, sometimes even refusal, to believe the horrors of the Nazi concentration camps that led General Eisenhower to order his troops to tour the camps.

"We are told that the American soldier does not know what he is fighting for," Eisenhower had said. "Now, at least, he will know what he is fighting against."

Decades later, there are still those who refuse to believe that the Holocaust happened. They claim that killing on that scale would have been impossible. Others say that details of the Holocaust are grossly exaggerated. Still others go so far as to suggest that the entire idea of the Holocaust is a conspiracy of propaganda started by Jewish people.

Thankfully, there were enough witnesses, like the liberating soldiers and General Eisenhower, and enough survivors, some of whose stories are told in this book, to prove the Holocaust deniers wrong. Many survivors and witnesses to the terror and horror of the battles of World War II as well as the Holocaust were reluctant to tell what they had seen. Some just wanted to forget, and others felt that nobody would want to hear such gruesome accounts.

Luckily, there were those who saw the importance of sharing the stories, no matter how difficult, and bringing both the truth of the Holocaust and the struggle of the battle to light. Now, sixty-five years after the end of World War II, fewer and fewer soldiers and survivors remain. Therefore, the stories they have left behind have become more and more valuable. In many ways, every little detail of the marches, the battles, the death camps, the victories, and the losses is a tribute to those who sacrificed so much.

"I decided to devote my life to telling the story because I felt that having survived, I owe something to the dead," explains Auschwitz survivor and author Elie Wiesel. "And anyone who does not remember betrays them again."